# Business Result

## Starter | Student's Book

John Hughes & Penny McLarty

Interactive Workbook material
by Chris Speck

D1501793

OXFORD
UNIVERSITY PRESS

# Contents

| | Introduction | 3 | | | | | |
|---|---|---|---|---|---|---|---|

| | | Working with words | Language at work | Practically speaking | Business communication | Activity | Outcomes – you can: |
|---|---|---|---|---|---|---|---|
| 1 | You **4–9** | Introducing yourself, jobs *My name's, What's your job?, finance director* | *I'm / you're / Are you …?* | Spelling | **Socializing** Meeting people **VIDEO** | Meeting people at a conference | • introduce yourself • talk about jobs • ask about names and jobs • spell • meet people |
| 2 | Company **10–15** | Companies and countries *I work for, Spain* **VIDEO** | *is / isn't* | Numbers 0–9 | **Telephoning** Starting a telephone call | The company game | • talk about companies and countries • ask about people and companies • say numbers 0–9 • start a telephone call |
| 3 | Workplace **16–21** | Your company *sales office, factory* **VIDEO** | *We / They are* *Wh-* questions | Email and website addresses | **Emails** Requests | What's the answer? | • talk about your company • ask questions • say email and website addresses • email a request |
| 4 | Departments **22–27** | Responsibilities and departments *manage, sell, Production, Logistics* **VIDEO** | Present simple: *I / you / we / they* | *there is / there are* | **Telephoning** Taking and leaving a message | Voicemail messages | • talk about responsibilities and departments • ask about people and departments • describe departments • take and leave a message |
| 5 | Products **28–33** | Company types and activities *automobile, electronics, buy, export* **VIDEO** | Present simple: *he / she / it* | Big numbers | **Telephoning** An order | The question game | • talk about company types and activities • ask about company products • say big numbers • order a product |
| 6 | Entertaining **34–39** | Food and drink *lunch, salad, I like* | *can / can't* | Days and times | **Socializing** Inviting, accepting and declining **VIDEO** | Making conversation in the restaurant | • talk about food and drink • talk about ability • say days and times • invite, accept and decline |
| 7 | Technology **40–45** | Office technology *laptop, webcam, scan, print* **VIDEO** | Possessive adjectives | *this, that, these, those* | **Exchanging information** Giving instructions | Guess the technology | • talk about office technology • talk about what's in your office • give instructions |
| 8 | Travel **46–51** | Transport and travel *train, car, check in, arrive* **VIDEO** | *was / were* | Months and dates | **Telephoning and emails** Arranging a meeting | When can we meet? | • talk about transport and travel • talk about the past • say months and dates • arrange a meeting |

| Revision game | 52–53 | Information files | 70–73 |
|---|---|---|---|
| Practice files | 54–69 | Audio scripts | 74–79 |

**VIDEO** : This section of the unit has a video clip linked to the topic.

# How to use Business Result Starter | A complete blended learning package

**In your *Business Result Starter Student's Book* pack:**
Student's Book; DVD-ROM; Access card to Business Result Starter Online Workbook

## In class

### Student's Book | Main unit

**Working with words**
Vocabulary

**Language at work**
Grammar

**Business communication**
Key expressions

**Practically speaking**
Everyday English

**Activity**
Fluency task or game

### Student's Book | Practice file

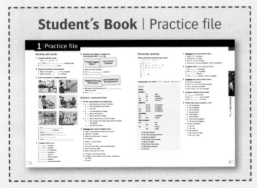

### Video + worksheets

## At home
### Interactive Workbook

**Online only**
Reading activities
Discussions

**Online & DVD-ROM**
Exercises | Tests | Email practice
Sample emails | Video
Glossaries | Class audio

**DVD-ROM only**
Phrasebank and
personal phrasebook

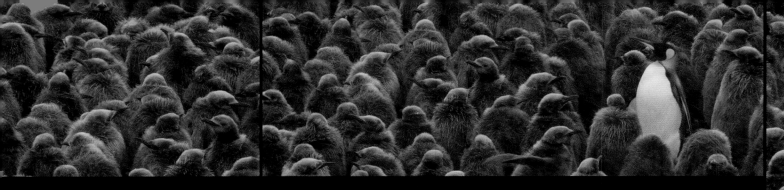

# 1 | You

**Learning objectives in this unit**
- Introducing yourself
- Talking about jobs
- Asking about names and jobs
- Alphabet and spelling
- Meeting people

**Activity**
- Meeting people at a conference

## Starting point

1 What's your name?

2 What's your job?

## Working with words | Introducing yourself | Jobs

**1** 01▷ **Listen and read.**

Hello, I'm Luis Moreira.

Hello, my name's Fabienne Mercier.

Hello, I'm Tageshi.

Hi, I'm Paula.

**2** 01▷ **Listen again and repeat.**

**3** **Work in pairs. Introduce yourself.**
*Examples: Hello, my name's (Sarah Kocian).*
*Hi, I'm (Yann).*

**4** **Stand up. Introduce yourself to other students.**

**5** 02▷ **Listen and read.**

1 IT technician

2 finance director

3 office assistant

4 sales representative

5 engineer

6 human resources manager

**6** 03▷ **Listen and repeat.**

● ●●    ●●●    ● ●●    ● ●● ●●    ●● ●    ● ●●

technician    director    assistant    representative    manager    engineer

**7** 04▷ **Listen and complete with a job from 5.**

**Fabienne**    I'm a ¹_____ _____ _____ . What's your job, Luis?
**Luis**    Oh, I'm a ²_____ _____ .

**Paula**    What's your job, Tageshi?
**Tageshi**    I'm an ³_____ _____ . And you?
**Paula**    I'm an ⁴_____ _____ .

**8** **Work in pairs. Practise the conversations in 7.**

➤➤ For more exercises, go to **Practice file 1** on page 54.

**9** **Work in pairs. Practise the conversations in 7 with your name and job.**

ⓘ ➤➤ Interactive Workbook ➤➤ Glossary

**Tip** | *a / an*
*a **m**anager*
*a **d**irector*
*an **a**ssistant*
*an **e**ngineer*

## Language at work | *I'm / you're / Are you ...?*

**1** 05▷ **Listen and read.**

| Jacob | Hi, I'm Jacob. |
| Kenji | I'm Kenji. Hello. |
| Jacob | And you're Alice. |
| Maria | No, I'm not Alice. I'm Maria. |
| Jacob | Sorry. You're Alice. |
| Alice | Yes. Hello. |

**2** **Complete with *'m* or *'re*.**

| Positive | Negative |
| --- | --- |
| I'm Jacob. | I _____ not Alice. |
| You _____ Alice. | You're not Maria. |

**3** **Work in groups of four. Practise the conversation in 1.**

**4** 06▷ **Listen and complete with the words.**

   *Are   'm not   'm   am*

| Jacob | ¹_____ you an office assistant? |
| Maria | Yes, I ²_____. Are you a human resources manager? |
| Jacob | No, I ³_____. I ⁴_____ a finance director. |

| Question | Short answers |
| --- | --- |
| Are you a director? | Yes, I am. |
| | No, I'm not. |

**5** **Work in pairs. Choose a job. Ask and answer questions.**

| office assistant | IT technician | human resources manager | finance director |

> *Examples:* **A** *Are you an office assistant?* **B** *Yes, I am.*
> **A** *Are you a finance director?* **B** *No, I'm not. I'm an IT technician.*

**Tip** | *'m / am, 're / are*
Use *'m* or *'re* for speaking:
   *I am = I'm*
   *You are = You're*
Use *am* for short answers:
   *Are you a manager?*
   *Yes, I am.*

▶▶ For more information and exercises, go to **Practice file 1** on page 55.

**6** 07▷ Listen and find the name badge.

1
**Tomas Gorski**
Technical Assistant

2
**Enzo Gonzales**
Sales Representative
OSB

3
**Enzo Silva**
Sales Manager

4
**Daisuke Hori**
IT Technician
AXi

**7** Work in pairs. Student A, choose a name badge in **6**. Answer Student B's questions. Student B, ask Student A questions. Find the name badge.

*Example: A* Are you Tomas?  *B* No, I'm not.
*A* Are you an IT technician?  *B* Yes, I am.
*A* You're Daisuke.  *B* Yes, I am.

## Practically speaking | Spelling

**1** 08▷ Listen and repeat.

A B C D E F G H I J K L M N O P Q R S T U V W X Y Z

**2** Work in pairs. Say the letters on the keyboard.

**3** 09▷ Listen and complete with the surname and first name.

| First name | Surname |
|---|---|
| Jane | Burton |
| Steven | 1_____ |
| 2_____ | Borysiak |

**4** Work in pairs. Spell the names in **3**.

*Example: A* Jane Burton.
*B* Can you spell that?
*A* J-A-N-E B-U-R-T-O-N.

▶▶ For more exercises, go to **Practice file 1** on page 55.

**5** Work in pairs. Ask and answer the questions. Write the names.

*What's your first name? Can you spell that?*
*What's your surname? Can you spell that?*

## Business communication | Meeting people

**1** 10▷ **Listen to three conversations. Match to the pictures.**

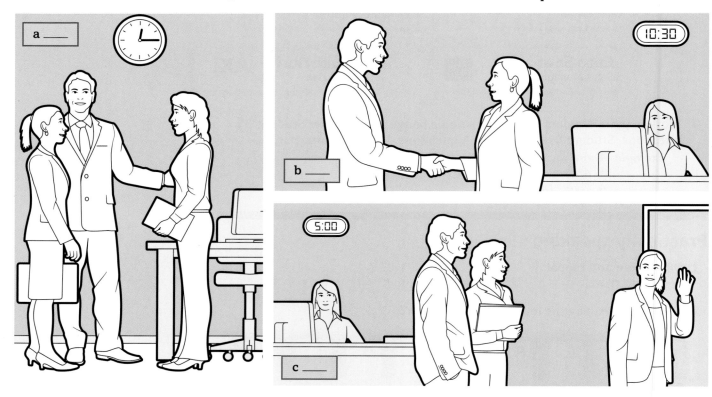

## Key expressions

**Saying hello**
Hello / Hi.
Good morning / afternoon / evening.

**Meeting people**
What's your name?
Are you (Mara)?
I'm (Jacob).
My name's (Naomi Sato).
Nice to meet you.
Nice to meet you too.

**Introducing other people**
This is (Alek).
This is my assistant.

**Saying goodbye**
Bye.
Goodbye.
See you soon.
It was nice meeting you.

ⓘ ❯❯ Interactive Workbook
❯❯ Phrasebank

**2** Match 1–5 to a–e.
1 Good morning. Are you Kasia? ___
2 I'm Franco. Nice to meet you. ___
3 This is Sally. ___
4 See you soon. ___
5 Goodbye. ___

a Good afternoon, Sally. Nice to meet you.
b Yes, I am.
c Yes, see you soon. And it was nice meeting you, Sally.
d Bye.
e Nice to meet you too.

**3** 11▷ Listen, check, and repeat.

**4** Put the expressions in **2** into the categories.
1 Say hello and meet people   _1b_   ___
2 Introduce other people ___
3 Say goodbye ___ ___

❯❯ For more exercises, go to **Practice file 1** on page 54.

**5** Work in groups of three. Look at the pictures in **1**. Practise the conversations. Use your own names if you want.
Student A  You are Franco.
Student B  You are Kasia.
Student C  You are Sally.

**6** Stand up. Say hello and meet people. Introduce other people. Say goodbye.

ⓘ ❯❯ Interactive Workbook ❯❯ **Email** and **Exercises and Tests**

## Meeting people at a conference

**1** Work in groups of three. You are at a conference. Student A is a conference manager. Complete the expressions and practise the conversation.

| STUDENT A | STUDENT B | STUDENT C |
|---|---|---|

Hello. _____ your name?

I'm _____ _____.

Can _____ spell that?

Yes, it's _____.

My name's _____. Nice to _____ _____.

_____ _____ meet you too.

This is _____.

_____ to meet _____.

Nice _____ _____ _____ too. My name's _____.

_____ your job?

I'm a _____. What's _____ _____?

I'm a _____.

It was nice _____ _____. See you _____.

Good_____!

_____bye!

**2** Change roles and repeat the conversation.

Activity

# 2 | Company

## Learning objectives in this unit

- Talking about companies and countries
- Asking about people and companies
- Saying numbers 0–9
- Starting a telephone call

### Activity

- The company game

## Starting point

1 What is on a business card? (e.g. name)

2 What is on your business card? Show the class.

## Working with words | Companies and countries

**1** 12▷ **Listen and read. Complete the business card.**

| | |
|---|---|
| **Saleh** | Hello. Are you Ricardo Ferreira? |
| **Ricardo** | Yes, I am. |
| **Saleh** | My name's Saleh Al-Banwan. I work for Zain. |
| **Ricardo** | Oh, nice to meet you. |
| **Saleh** | I'm an engineer in the head office in Kuwait. Here's my card. |

Dr Saleh Al-Banwan
Network [1]E_____
[2]Z_____
Head Office, Airport Road, 13083 Safat
[3]_____

**2** 13▷ **Listen and complete the business cards with the companies.**

*Asiana Airlines   Petrobras   Santander*

Alex Rivers
Manager
[1]_____

Spain

Jae Min Park
Marketing Assistant
[2]_____

South Korea

Ricardo Ferreira
Engineer
[3]_____

Rio de Janeiro

**3** Work in pairs. Practise the conversation.

    **A** *Hello. I work for _____ . What's your company?*

    **B** *My company is _____ .*

**4** Work in pairs. Look at the map. Where is your head office?

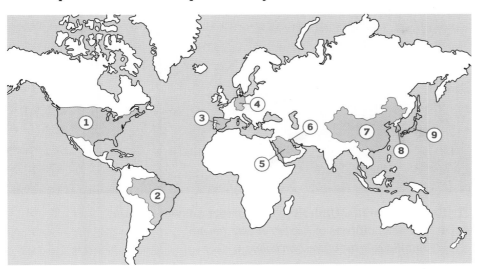

**5** Look at the map again. Find the countries.

●    ●●    ●●    ●●    ● ●    ● ●●    ● ●●●    ● ●● ●● 

Spain    China    Brazil    Japan    Kuwait    Germany    South Korea    the USA    Saudi Arabia

**6** 14▷ Listen and repeat the countries in **5**.

**7** 15▷ Listen and complete with the countries.

|  | Saleh | Alex | Jae Min | Ricardo |
|---|---|---|---|---|
| Where are you from? | *Saudi Arabia* |  |  |  |
| Where's your company / head office? |  |  |  |  |

**8** 15▷ Listen again. Complete the questions and answers.

  1   Where are you from, Saleh?      _____ _____ Saudi Arabia.

  2   _____ your company?      My _____ is Santander.

  3   _____ your head office?      It's in Seoul.

  4   _____ are you from, Ricardo?      I'm from Brazil and I _____ for Petrobras.

**9** Complete the sentences about you.

    I'm from _____ .

    I work for / My company is _____ .

    My head office is in _____ .

**10** Work in pairs. Ask and answer.

    Where are you from?    What's your company?    Where's your head office?

  ▶▶ For more exercises, go to **Practice file 2** on page 56.

**11** Work in pairs. Student A, turn to File 7 on page 71. Student B, turn to File 12 on page 72.

ⓘ ▶▶ Interactive Workbook ▶▶ Glossary

**Tip** | *and*

*My company is Santander.*
*Our head office is in Spain. =*
*My company is Santander **and**
our head office is in Spain.*

## Language at work | *is / isn't*

**1** Read the emails. <u>Underline</u> the correct answer in *italics*.

1 The head office is in *Recife / Rio de Janeiro*.

2 Camilla is *in the office / on holiday*.

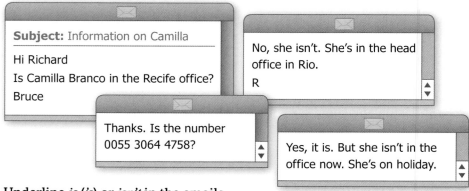

**Subject:** Information on Camilla

Hi Richard

Is Camilla Branco in the Recife office?

Bruce

No, she isn't. She's in the head office in Rio.

R

Thanks. Is the number 0055 3064 4758?

Yes, it is. But she isn't in the office now. She's on holiday.

**2** <u>Underline</u> *is* (*'s*) or *isn't* in the emails.

**3** Complete with *is* (*'s*) or *isn't*.

| Positive | Negative | Questions | Short answers |
|---|---|---|---|
| He / She / It _____ in the office. | He / She / It _____ in Recife. | _____ he / she / it in Rio? | Yes, he / she / it _____ . No, he / she / it _____ . |

**4** 16▷ Complete with *is* (*'s*) or *isn't*. Listen and check.

**A** Hello, I work for Oltecha.

**B** Nice to meet you. My company [1]_____ Petrobras.

**A** [2]_____ your head office in São Paulo?

**B** No, it [3]_____ . It's in Rio. Where's your company?

**A** I work in São Paulo and the company head office [4]_____ in Stavanger.

**B** [5]_____ Stavanger in Norway?

**A** Yes, it [6]_____ .

**5** Work in pairs. Practise the conversation in **4**.

>> For more information and exercises, go to **Practice file 2** on page 57.

**Tip** | *'s* or *is*?
Use *'s* for speaking:
  *He's = He is*
  *Camilla's = Camilla is*

**6** **Work in pairs. Student A, see below. Student B, turn to File 16 on page 73.**
**Student A**

1 Look at the map. Ask Student B about Ricardo, Lokas, and Chen.
  *Example: **A** Is Ricardo in the Portugal office?*     ***B** No, he isn't.*
  *          **A** Is he in the Brazil office?*     ***B** Yes, he is.*

2 Answer Student B about Rachel, Maya, and Alex.

Ricardo, Petrobras

Lokas, Oltecha

Chen, Shell

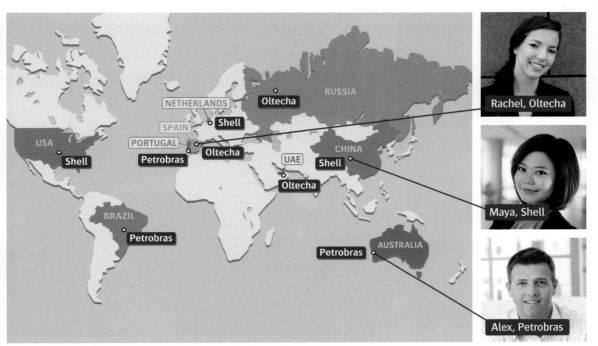

NETHERLANDS
SPAIN
USA
Shell
PORTUGAL
Petrobras
Oltecha
RUSSIA
Oltecha
Shell
UAE
CHINA
Shell
Oltecha
BRAZIL
Petrobras
Petrobras
AUSTRALIA

Rachel, Oltecha

Maya, Shell

Alex, Petrobras

---

## Practically speaking | Numbers 0–9

**1** **17▷ Read, listen, and repeat the numbers on the telephone.**

**2** **18▷ Listen and circle the numbers on the telephone.**

**3** **19▷ Listen and complete the passcode on the telephone.**

**4** **20▷ Listen and complete the numbers.**
  1 Flight BA 3___10      3 Credit card number 41___2 ___409 37___8 2___58
  2 Security code ___82___    4 Passport number 6___42___87___2

  **»** For more exercises, go to **Practise file 2** on page 57.

Passcode

| 1 | 2 | 3 |
| 4 | 5 | 6 |
| 7 | 8 | 9 |
| * | 0 | # |

**5** **Complete the table for you.**

| Numbers | You | Your partner |
|---|---|---|
| Work | | |
| Extension | | |
| Mobile | | |

**Tip | Saying numbers**

| 0 | oh / zero | 5 | five |
| 1 | one | 6 | six |
| 2 | two | 7 | seven |
| 3 | three | 8 | eight |
| 4 | four | 9 | nine |

**6** **Work in pairs. Say your numbers. Write your partner's numbers in the table.**
  *My work number is …   My extension number is …*

## Business communication | Starting a telephone call

**1** 21▷ **Listen to a telephone call. Is Aitur Garitano there?**

**2** 21▷ **Listen again. Put the conversation in the right order (1, 2, 3, 4).**

*1* Good morning. Inditex Spain.
___ Yes, of course. One moment.
___ Thanks.
___ Good morning. Can I speak to Aitur Garitano, please?

**3** **Work in pairs. Practise the conversation in 2.**

**4** 22▷ **Listen to two telephone calls. Is Rosa in the office? Tick (✓) YES or NO.**
Conversation 1     YES ☐     NO ☐
Conversation 2     YES ☐     NO ☐

**5** 22▷ **Listen again. Match questions 1–3 to responses a–c.**

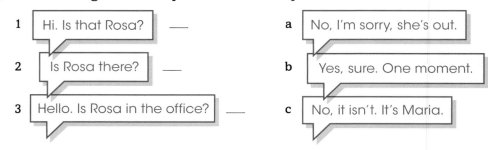

1  Hi. Is that Rosa?  ___    a  No, I'm sorry, she's out.

2  Is Rosa there?  ___    b  Yes, sure. One moment.

3  Hello. Is Rosa in the office?  ___    c  No, it isn't. It's Maria.

>> For more exercises, go to **Practice file 2** on page 56.

**6** **Work in pairs. Take turns. Start and answer a telephone call to the people in the pictures.**

*Example:* **A** *Good morning, Markus speaking.*
**B** *Hello. Is Sophia there?*
**A** *No, I'm sorry, she's not in the office.*
**B** *OK. Thanks.*

---

## Key expressions

**Starting a call**
Good morning / afternoon.
Hello / Hi.

**Answering a call**
Good morning, (company name).
(Maria) speaking.

**Asking for someone**
Can I speak to (Aitur Garitano), please?
Hello. Is (Rosa) there?
Is (Alek) in the office?
Is that (Lukas)?

**Saying 'yes'**
Yes, of course. (One moment.)
Sure. (One moment.)

**Saying 'no'**
No, I'm sorry, she's not in the office.
No, I'm sorry, he's out.
No, it isn't. It's (Clara).

**Ending a call**
OK. Thanks.
Goodbye.

*ⓘ* **»** Interactive Workbook
   **» Phrasebank**

*ⓘ* **»** Interactive Workbook **»** **Email** and **Exercises and Tests**

# The company game

**Work in pairs. Make five conversations.**

1 Start on pink . Choose a square.

2 Move to green . Then blue . Then yellow .

3 Practise the conversation.

4 Choose a new pink square. Make a new conversation.

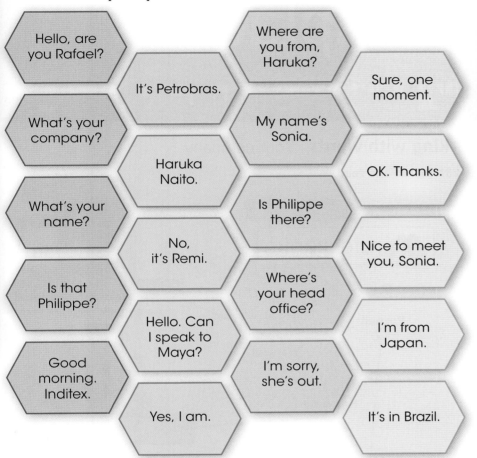

Hello, are you Rafael?

Where are you from, Haruka?

It's Petrobras.

Sure, one moment.

What's your company?

My name's Sonia.

Haruka Naito.

OK. Thanks.

What's your name?

Is Philippe there?

No, it's Remi.

Nice to meet you, Sonia.

Is that Philippe?

Where's your head office?

Hello. Can I speak to Maya?

I'm from Japan.

Good morning. Inditex.

I'm sorry, she's out.

Yes, I am.

It's in Brazil.

Activity

# 3 | Workplace

**Learning objectives in this unit**

- Talking about your company
- Asking questions
- Saying email and website addresses
- Emailing a request

**Activity**

- What's the answer?

## Starting point

**Where is**

- your company?
- the head office?
- your office?

## Working with words | Your company

**1** 23▷ **Listen and read.**

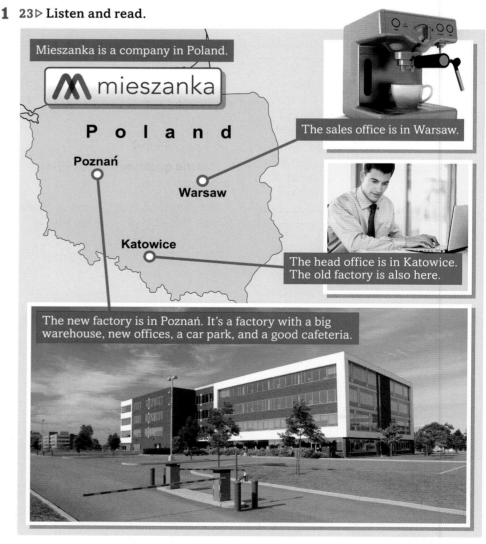

Mieszanka is a company in Poland.

mieszanka

**P o l a n d**

Poznań

Warsaw

Katowice

The sales office is in Warsaw.

The head office is in Katowice. The old factory is also here.

The new factory is in Poznań. It's a factory with a big warehouse, new offices, a car park, and a good cafeteria.

**2** Where is

1 Mieszanka?
2 the head office?
3 the sales office?
4 the new factory?

**3** Match the words to the pictures.

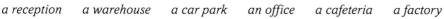
*a reception*     *a warehouse*     *a car park*     *an office*     *a cafeteria*     *a factory*

1 _____  2 _____  3 _____

4 _____  5 _____  6 _____

**4** 24▷ **Listen and repeat.**

● ● ● ●● ●●●●● ●●● ●● ● ●
a warehouse   a factory   a cafeteria   a reception   an office   a car park

**5** Work in pairs. What places in **3** are in your company?

**6** Look at the adjectives below then answer the questions about Mieszanka.

Adjectives

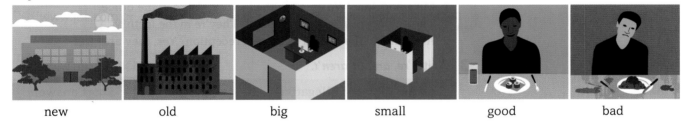

new          old          big          small          good          bad

1  Is the factory in Katowice old or new?
2  Is the warehouse in Poznań big or small?
3  Is the cafeteria in Poznań good or bad?

**7** 25▷ **Listen to three people. Complete with the adjectives.**
1  The sales office in London is _____ .
2  The factory and warehouse are _____ , but they are _____ .
3  The cafeteria is _____ , but the food is _____ .

▶▶ For more exercises, go to **Practice file 3** on page 58.

**8** Work in pairs. Talk about places at work using adjectives.
   *Example: My office is old.*
   • your office            • the car park            • the cafeteria (or café)
   • your head office       • other places (e.g. the warehouse)

ⓘ ▶▶ Interactive Workbook ▶▶ Glossary

**Tip** | Adjective + noun
*The office is new. = It's a
new office.*
NOT *It's ~~an office new.~~*

17

## Business communication | Requests

**1** **Read emails 1 and 2. Answer the questions.**

1 Where is the visit?    2 What is the request?

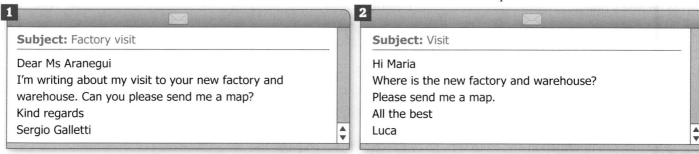

**1**

**Subject:** Factory visit

Dear Ms Aranegui

I'm writing about my visit to your new factory and warehouse. Can you please send me a map?

Kind regards

Sergio Galletti

**2**

**Subject:** Visit

Hi Maria

Where is the new factory and warehouse?

Please send me a map.

All the best

Luca

**2** **Match emails 3 and 4 to emails 1 and 2.**

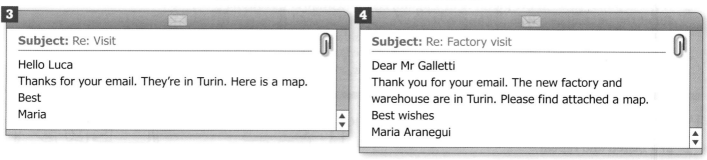

**3**

**Subject:** Re: Visit

Hello Luca

Thanks for your email. They're in Turin. Here is a map.

Best

Maria

**4**

**Subject:** Re: Factory visit

Dear Mr Galletti

Thank you for your email. The new factory and warehouse are in Turin. Please find attached a map.

Best wishes

Maria Aranegui

**3** **Complete with the phrases.**

*Thank you for    Hi    Can you please send    Kind regards*
*Where is    All the best    I'm writing about    Here is    Dear*

| Emails 1 and 4 | Emails 2 and 3 |
|---|---|
| _____ Ms Aranegui / Mr Galletti | _____ Maria / Hello Luca |
| _____ my visit to your new factory … | _____ the new factory …? |
| _____ | Thanks for |
| _____ | Please send |
| Please find attached | _____ |
| Best wishes / _____ | _____ / Best |

**4** **Which two emails are formal?**

>> For more exercises, go to **Practice file 3** on page 58.

**5** **Complete the emails with phrases from 3.**

1 _____ Taro
Where's the meeting?
2 _____ me details.
Best
Keita

3 _____ Mr Nakamura
4 _____ the meeting at the sales office. Can you please send me details?
5 _____
Miki Shiratori

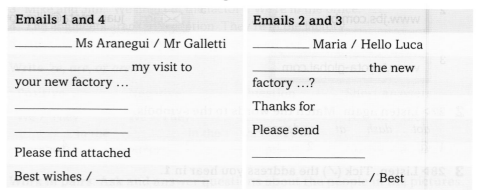

### Key expressions

**Opening**
Hello / Hi
Dear Mr / Mrs / Ms*

**Previous contact**
Thank you for (your email).*
Thanks for (your email).

**Reason for writing**
I'm writing about …*

**Requesting**
Please send …
Can you please send …*

**Attachments**
Please find attached (a map).*
Here is (a map).

**Closing**
Best wishes / Kind regards*
All the best / Best

* formal phrases

ⓘ >> Interactive Workbook
>> **Phrasebank**

ⓘ >> Interactive Workbook >> **Email** and **Exercises and Tests**

# What's the answer?

**Work in pairs or teams. Student A / Team A, see below.**
**Student B / Team B, turn to File 15 on page 73.**
Ask and answer questions.

**Team A**

1  Choose a blue question square.
2  Ask Student B / Team B your question.

**Team B**

1  Find the correct yellow answer square.
2  Answer the question.
3  Choose a blue question square. Ask Student A / Team A your question.

**Student A / Team A**

| | | | |
|---|---|---|---|
| Yes, she is. | Is the factory in Russia? | It's in Lima. | Where are the offices? |
| Are they in reception? | It's old. | Where is Simon? | Yes, it is. |

Activity

# 4 | Departments

**Learning objectives in this unit**
- Talking about responsibilities and departments
- Asking about people and departments
- Describing departments
- Taking and leaving a message

**Activity**
- Voicemail messages

## Starting point

1 Are you in a department?

2 What's your department?

3 In your department, are you
- in a team?
- on your own?

**Tip** | Talking about big numbers

= 300 *three hundred*
> 300 *more than / over 300*
< 300 *less than / under 300*

## Working with words | Responsibilities and departments

**1** 30▷ **Listen and read.**

My name's Joanna. I'm from Hungary and I live in Sopron. I work for a software company. We make CD-ROMs and DVDs. I'm a sales rep and I meet customers. I sell the products to training companies and schools. We have three people in the Sales Department. I work in West Hungary and Austria.

My name's Fred Meesmaecker. I'm from France, but I live in England. I work for Capgemini. It's a global company. We have over 300 offices in more than 40 countries. I'm a project manager and I manage a team of IT technicians. I have eight people in my team and they manage computer systems for the client. This month, we have a project with a food company.

**2** Complete the table about the people in **1**.

| Name | Home | Job | What you do | Number of people in team or department |
|------|------|-----|-------------|----------------------------------------|
| Joanna | | Sales rep | | 3 |
| | England | | Manage a team | |

**3** Underline the verbs in the texts in **1**.

**4** Complete with the verbs.

*work    live    make    manage    meet    have    sell*

My name's Deshi and I'm a sales manager. I'm from China, but I ¹_____ in Seattle in the USA. I ²_____ for URF Solutions. We're an IT company and we ³_____ websites for companies. I ⁴_____ the Sales Department. I ⁵_____ six people in my team. They ⁶_____ customers and they ⁷_____ the products to companies in North America.

**5** 31▷ **Listen and repeat the verbs from 4.**

**6** Write about you with the verbs in **4**, then tell your partner.

**7** 32▷ **Look at the departments in the company. Listen and repeat the departments.**

Andreas

| Logistics | Sales | Production | IT | Finance | Human Resources |
|---|---|---|---|---|---|
| Carl and Dan | Greta | Carlos | Antony | Anne-Marie | Ilse |

**8** Who from **7** says 1–7?
1  We make the products. _____
2  I have three people in my team. They sell the products. _____
3  We manage transport. _____
4  I manage the computer system. _____
5  I manage the company. We have six departments. _____
6  I meet new employees. _____
7  I work on my own. I manage money. _____

**9** 33▷ **Find the plural form of these words on pages 22 and 23. Then listen and repeat.**

department  _departments_     customer _____     product _____
company _____     office _____     technician _____
employee _____     person _____     country _____

≫ For more exercises, go to **Practice file 4** on page 60.

**10** Draw your company structure with the names of six departments. Show your partner and talk about the departments.
    ***Example:*** *We have a (sales) department. They (make / sell / manage / have) …*

ⓘ ≫ Interactive Workbook ≫ Glossary

**Tip** | Plural form
For most nouns, add -s:
department → departments
For nouns ending in -y, change to -ies:
company → companies
Some plural nouns are irregular: person → **people**

## Language at work | Present simple: *I / you / we / they*

**1** 34▷ **Karla is a manager. Today, she is with two new employees. Listen and match the person to the department.**

| | |
|---|---|
| Karla | Sales |
| Astrid | Human Resources |
| Mark | Finance |

**2** 34▷ **Listen again. Complete with the words.**

*work (x2)    don't (x2)    do (x2)    manage    live*

1  I _____ the Human Resources Department.
2  I'm from Switzerland, but I _____ live there.
3  We _____ in Munich.
4  Do you _____ in Sales?
5  Yes, I _____ .
6  What _____ you do?
7  I _____ in Finance.
8  No, I _____ . I live in Canada.

**3** **Complete with *do* or *don't*.**

| Positive | Negative | Question | Short answers |
|---|---|---|---|
| I / you / we / they manage a department. | I / you / we / they _____ work in Sales. | _____ you / they live in Germany? | Yes, I / we / they _____ . No, I / we / they _____ . |

**4** **Work in pairs. Make six questions.**

| | | |
|---|---|---|
| | manage | a department? |
| | live in | Spain? |
| Do you | work in | people? |
| | meet | a team? |
| | sell | products? |
| | make | India? |

**5** **Work in pairs. Ask the questions from 4. Answer *Yes, I do* or *No, I don't*.**

24

**6** Complete with *Who*, *What*, or *Where*.

1 _____ do you do?

2 _____ do you work for?

3 _____ do you live?

**7** Work in pairs. Make questions for these answers using the questions from **6**.

*Example: A What do you do?  B I'm a production manager.*

I'm a production manager.

We live in Lima.

We manage training courses.

We work for a small IT company.

I work for Alcatel-Lucent.

I make computers.

I'm an engineer.

I sell products.

>> For more information and exercises, go to **Practice file 4** on page 61.

**8** Stand up! Meet other people. Ask and answer the questions in **6**.

## Practically speaking | *there is / there are*

**1** Read about a department. <u>Underline</u> the verbs.

There are four people in my department. There's a manager at head office. There are two IT technicians and there's an assistant.

**2** Complete the table with two verbs.

| There | _____ | a / an<br>one | manager.<br>assistant. |
|---|---|---|---|
| There | _____ | two<br>four | technicians.<br>people. |

**3** Complete with *'s* or *are*.

1 There _____ 200 offices in 30 countries.

2 There _____ an office in London.

3 There _____ 18 offices in the UK.

4 There _____ a Human Resources Department.

>> For more exercises, go to **Practice file 4** on page 61.

**4** Work in pairs. Talk about your company and your department using *there is / there are*. Talk about

• offices and countries

• departments

• people and jobs in your department or team.

**Tip** | *What do you do?*
*What do you do?* =
*What's your job?*

25

## Business communication | Taking and leaving a message

**1** Do you call people in other departments? Which departments?

**2** 35▷ Listen to a telephone conversation. Complete the message.

> **Message for:** _Liko_
> **Caller:** _Janusz in the_ ¹_____ _Department_
> **Reason for call:** _the new_ ²_____ _website_
> _____
> **Message:**
>    _Do you want www.synox-sales.com or www.synox-sales_ ³_____
>    _Call Janusz on this number:_ ⁴_____

**3** 35▷ Listen again and complete the conversation.

**Martha** Sales. Hello?

**Janusz** Hi. Is Liko there?

**Martha** No, I'm sorry, he's out. Can I take ¹_____ _____?

**Janusz** Yes, it's Janusz in IT.

**Martha** Oh, hi. This is Martha. I'm the new sales assistant.

**Janusz** Hi, Martha. ²_____ _____ about the new sales website.

**Martha** Sorry, one moment. OK. ³_____ _____. What's the message for Liko?

**Janusz** It's about the sales website. Do you want dot com or dot co dot uk in the address?

**Martha** Sorry, I ⁴_____ understand. Can you ⁵_____ that?

**Janusz** The new website is www.synox-sales, but do you want synox-sales dot com or synox-sales dot co dot uk?

**Martha** OK. ⁶_____ _____ anything else?

**Janusz** Yes. Please ⁷_____ me _____ as soon as possible. My mobile number is 07700 897 833.

**Martha** So that's 07700 897 833.

**Janusz** That's right.

**Martha** OK. I'll ⁸_____ Liko your _____.

**Janusz** Thanks, Martha.

**4** Work in pairs. Practise the conversation in **3**.

>> For more exercises, go to **Practice file 4** on page 60.

**5** Work in pairs. Practise two telephone conversations. Student A, turn to File 01 on page 70. Student B, turn to File 06 on page 71.

ⓘ >> Interactive Workbook >> **Email** and **Exercises and Tests**

## Key expressions

**Taking a message**
Can I take a message?
Go ahead.

**Leaving a message**
I'm calling about (the new website).
It's about (the sales website).
Please call me back as soon as possible.
My number is (07700 897 833).

**Asking for repetition and checking**
Sorry, I don't understand.
Can you repeat that?
So that's (07700 897 833).

**Ending the call**
Is there anything else?
I'll give (Liko) your message.

ⓘ >> Interactive Workbook
>> **Phrasebank**

## Voicemail messages

**1** **Read about a company. Answer the questions.**

**SYNOX**

Synox Solutions is an IT company. There are two offices in Europe and one office in the Middle East. The head office is in Bristol in England. They have projects with clients in Europe and the Middle East. They manage computer systems and write new software. There are 25 people in the head office. There are departments for Human Resources and Sales. They also have teams of IT technicians for projects.

1  Where is the head office of Synox Solutions?
2  What do they do?
3  What are the departments?
4  Is it a big company?

**2**  **36▷ You work for Synox Solutions. Listen to three voicemails on the company phone. Complete the messages.**

Caller: ..............................................
Reason for call: ..............................................
Message:

Caller: ..............................................
Reason for call: ..............................................
Message:

Caller: ..............................................
Reason for call: ..............................................
Message:

**3**  **Work in pairs. Read the names and numbers of people in head office. Who do you give the messages in 2 to?**

| Name | Department | Extension |
|---|---|---|
| Olaf Pederson | Managing Director | 100 |
| Frank Rogers | IT Projects Manager | 101 |
| Ray Searle-Jones | IT Projects Assistant | 102 |
| Shaun Manus | Sales (Europe) | 104 |
| Tyler Khan-Yates | Sales (Middle East) | 105 |
| Emily Sanchez | HR Manager | 106 |
| Gill Reeves | HR Assistant | 107 |

**4**  **Tell the class your answers.**

Activity

# 5 | Products

**Learning objectives in this unit**

- Talking about company types and activities
- Asking about company products
- Saying big numbers
- Ordering a product

**Activity**

- The question game

## Starting point

**1** What does Microsoft make and sell?

**2** Does your company
- make a product?
- sell a product?

**3** What product does it
- make?
- sell?

## Working with words | Company types and activities

**1** 37▷ **Look at the pictures and listen.**

1 Gazprom / energy

2 Dassault / aeronautical

3 Aldi / retail

4 Toyota / automobile

5 Samsung / electronics

**2** 37▷ **Listen again. Complete with the words.**

*cars    oil and gas    televisions and mobiles    food    aeroplanes*

|         | Company type | Products |
|---------|--------------|----------|
| Gazprom | energy       |          |
| Dassault| aeronautical |          |
| Aldi    | retail       |          |
| Toyota  | automobile   |          |
| Samsung | electronics  |          |

**3** **Work in pairs. Choose a company from 1. Ask and answer.**

***Example:*** *A  I work for Aldi.*
           *A  It's a retail company.*
           *A  We sell food.*
           *B  What type of company is it?*
           *B  What do you do?*

**4** 38▷ **Listen and read. What type of company are Embraer and Uniqlo?**

Embraer is a Brazilian company. We make and sell aeroplanes. We have factories in Brazil and sales offices all over the world. In the factories we **build** aeroplanes. We also **design** new products by computer in the R&D* Department. We **export** products to China, the USA, and Europe.

* R&D = Research and Development

Uniqlo is a Japanese company. We sell clothes. We have stores in 13 countries around the world. Customers visit the stores and **buy** the products. We also have an online store. Customers **order** products online. Then we **deliver** the products to the customer.

**5** Match the verbs highlighted in **4** to the pictures.

    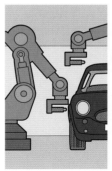 

1 _____  2 _____  3 _____  4 _____  5 _____  6 _____

**6** 39▷ **Listen, check, and repeat.**

**7** <u>Underline</u> the correct verb in *italics*.
1 We *export / build* cars in factories in Europe.
2 We *design / buy* new products in the R&D Department.
3 Customers visit the store and *build / buy* clothes.
4 We also have an online store. Customers *order / deliver* products online.
5 We *buy / deliver* the products to the customer.

>> For more exercises, go to **Practice file 5** on page 62.

**8** **Choose five verbs. Write five sentences about your company.**
   make   sell   have   build   design   buy   export   order   deliver
   ***Examples:*** *We make and sell _____ . We have _____ factories / stores.*

**9** **Present your company to the class.**

ⓘ >> Interactive Workbook >> **Glossary**

**Tip** | Countries and nationalities
the UK → British
Brazil → Brazilian
Italy → Italian
India → Indian
Mexico → Mexican
Japan → Japanese
the USA → American
China → Chinese

## Language at work | Present simple: *he / she / it*

**1**  40▷ **Listen and read.**

**2**  **Complete the table.**

Auchan is a retail company. It sells food and clothes. It has stores in Europe and Asia. The head office is in Croix, France. Martin Reuland works for Auchan, but he doesn't work in the head office. He is a store manager in Calais.

LG is an electronics company. It makes and sells televisions and mobile phones. Soo Jin Lee works in the R&D Department in Seoul. She designs new products. LG has over 20 factories in eleven countries and exports products all over the world.

|        | Type of company | Products |
|--------|-----------------|----------|
| Auchan |                 |          |
| LG     |                 |          |

**3**  <u>Underline</u> the verbs in the texts in **1**.

**4**  **Complete with** *-s, does,* **or** *doesn't*.

| Positive | Negative | Question | Short answers |
|----------|----------|----------|---------------|
| He / she / it sell_____ food products. | He / she / it _____ design new products. | _____ he / she / it make products? | Yes, he / she / it _____ . No, he / she / it _____ . |

**5**  **Complete the sentences with the correct form of the verbs in (brackets).**

1  Auchan _____ (sell) food and clothes.
2  He _____ (not work) in the head office.
3  LG _____ (have) over 20 factories in eleven countries.
4  She _____ (design) new products.
5  It _____ (export) products all over the world.
6  LG _____ (not make) food products.

**Tip** | *have / has*
We write *I / you / we / they have* but *he / she / it has*:
  It **has** stores all over the world.

**6** **Put the words in the right order.**

1 Martin / work / Does / Croix / in _____?

2 export / LG / products / Does _____?

3 Auchan / have / stores / Africa / in / Does _____?

4 design / Soo Jin Lee / new / Does / products _____?

5 she / work / the Sales Department / Does / in _____?

**7** **Match the answers to the questions in 6.**

a No, it doesn't. ___

b Yes, she does. ___

c No, he doesn't. ___

d Yes, it does. ___

e No, she doesn't. ___

**8** **41▷ Listen and check.**

**9** **Complete the question words.**

1 Wh_____ does Martin work?

2 Wh_____ does Soo Jin work for?

3 Wh_____ does LG export?

**10** **Match the questions to the answers.**

1 What does Auchan sell? ___

2 Where does Soo Jin work? ___

3 What does Martin do? ___

4 What does LG export? ___

5 Who does Martin work for? ___

a He's a store manager.

b It sells food and clothes.

c It exports televisions and mobile phones.

d He works for Auchan.

e She works in the R&D Department.

>> For more information and exercises, go to **Practice file 5** on page 63.

**11** **Work in pairs. Student A, turn to File 03 on page 70. Student B, turn to File 09 on page 71.**

## Practically speaking | Big numbers

**1** **42▷ Listen and repeat.**

| 10 | 11 | 12 | 13 | 14 | 15 | 16 | 17 | 18 | 19 |
|----|----|----|----|----|----|----|----|----|----|
| 20 | 30 | 40 | 50 | 60 | 70 | 80 | 90 | 100 | 1,000 |

**2** **Work in pairs. Take turns. Choose six numbers.**
**Student A, say your numbers. Student B, listen and write the numbers.**

**3** **43▷ Listen and repeat.**

27    82    145    610    3,900    21,340    172,000    58,000,000

**4** **44▷ Listen and write the numbers.**

1 _____    3 _____

2 _____    4 _____ _____

>> For more exercises, go to **Practice file 5** on page 63.

**5** **Work in pairs. Answer with numbers.**

1 The number of employees:   in your office / in your company

2 The population of:   your town / your city / your country

www.euroboxes.com

**EURO**BOXES

Euroboxes delivers cardboard boxes to businesses. We sell standard cardboard boxes but we also design packaging for your needs.

## Business communication | An order

**1  Read about a company.**

What does it sell? Does it deliver the products?

**2  45▷ Carel Peeters from Belgium calls Paul Rice at Euroboxes. Listen and complete the order form.**

| Product | Size | Item No | Price per box | Quantity | Total price |
|---------|------|---------|---------------|----------|-------------|
| SSW box | Small | 1 _____ - _____ | 20 cents | 2 _____ | 3 _____ euros |
| SSW box | Medium | 4 _____ - _____ | 5 _____ cents | 5,000 | 6 _____ euros |
|  |  |  |  |  | 7 _____ euros |

**3  Who says the phrases from the conversation? Tick (✓) *Company* or *Customer*.**

|  | Company | Customer |
|---|---------|----------|
| 1  Can I help you? | ☐ | ☐ |
| 2  I'd like to order Standard Single Wall boxes. | ☐ | ☐ |
| 3  Do you have the item number? | ☐ | ☐ |
| 4  How many would you like? | ☐ | ☐ |
| 5  Does that include delivery? | ☐ | ☐ |
| 6  And I also want 5,000 medium. | ☐ | ☐ |
| 7  What's the price? | ☐ | ☐ |
| 8  The total price is 3,250 euros. | ☐ | ☐ |
| 9  Can you confirm my order by email? | ☐ | ☐ |
| 10  I'll email that now. | ☐ | ☐ |

**4  45▷ Listen again and check.**

》 For more exercises, go to **Practice file 5** on page 62.

**5  Work in pairs. Practise a conversation between Paul Rice and a new customer.**

**Student A**  You are Paul Rice. Answer the phone and speak to the customer. The prices of boxes are: 20 cents (small), 25 cents (medium), 30 cents (large).

**Student B**  You are a customer. Order boxes: 7,500 small, 5,000 medium, 2,500 large. Ask for the total price.

ⓘ 》 Interactive Workbook 》 **Email** and **Exercises and Tests**

## Key expressions

**Ordering items**
I'd like to order (small Standard Single Wall boxes).
Do you have the item number?
The item number is (SSW-3411).
How many would you like?
I also want (5,000 medium).

**Talking about the price**
What's the price?
Does that include delivery?
The total price is (3,250 euros).

**Asking to confirm**
Can you confirm my order by email?
What's your email?
I'll email that now.

ⓘ 》 Interactive Workbook
》 **Phrasebank**

# The question game

**Work in pairs. Look at the three topics.**

1 Student A, ask Student B questions about Topic 1 (You). You have 5 minutes. Student B, tick (✓) a point for each correct question about Topic 1. Answer the question.
2 Change roles and repeat 1.
3 Repeat the activity for Topic 2 (Work) and Topic 3 (A company).
4 At the end, count all your points. What is your total? Who is the winner?

## Topics

### Topic 1 | You
- your name
- your country
- your job
- other?

### Topic 2 | Work
- your workplace
- your department
- your responsibilities
- other?

### Topic 3 | A company
- head office and offices
- location
- products and services
- other?

| Questions | Topic 1 Points | Topic 2 Points | Topic 3 Points |
|---|---|---|---|
| What's / What are …? | | | |
| Are you …? | | | |
| Is your company …? | | | |
| Where's / Where are …? | | | |
| Who is / Who are …? | | | |
| Do you …? | | | |
| Does your company …? | | | |
| What do …? | | | |
| What does …? | | | |
| Where do …? | | | |
| Where does …? | | | |
| What products do …? | | | |
| What products does …? | | | |
| What services do …? | | | |
| What services does …? | | | |
| Can you spell …? | | | |

**Total points:**

Activity

# 6 | Entertaining

- Talking about food and drink
- Talking about ability
- Saying days and times
- Inviting, accepting and declining

**Activity**

- Making conversation in the restaurant

## Starting point

1 **At work, do you eat lunch**
   - at your desk?
   - in the company cafeteria?
   - in a café or restaurant?

2 **What do you eat?**

## Working with words | Food and drink

1 Read the lunch menu in a company cafeteria. Match the pictures to the items in the menu.

### LUNCH MENU

**MEAT DISHES**
Steak and fries          $7.50
Chicken curry and rice   $6.50

**VEGETARIAN DISHES**
Vegetable lasagne        $6.50
Tomato soup with bread   $4.50
Salad                    $4.00
Cheese sandwich          $4.50

**DESSERTS**
Chocolate cake           $4.00
Ice cream                $3.00

**DRINKS**
Mineral water, Orange juice, Coffee, Tea
All drinks               $1.50

1 _____

2 _____

3 _____

4 _____

5 _____

6 _____

7 _____

8 _____

9 _____

10 _____

11 _____

12 _____

**Tip** | Saying prices
*$10.00 = ten dollars*
*$10.50 = ten dollars fifty*
*$0.50 = fifty cents*

**2**  46▷ **Listen, check, and repeat.**

**3**  47▷ **Mr Shimura is a visitor. He's in the company cafeteria with Mr Jarvis. Listen to the conversation. Are the sentences true (*T*) or false (*F*)?**
1  Mr Shimura wants steak and fries with salad. ___
2  Mr Jarvis wants chicken curry and rice. ___
3  Mr Jarvis would like chocolate cake. ___
4  They want coffee. ___
5  The total price is $23. ___

**4**  47▷ **Listen again. Number the sentences in the right order (1–5).**
**a** ___  What would you like?
**b** ___  I'd like steak and fries with salad.
**c** ___  Hello, can I help you?
**d** ___  That's $23, please.
**e** ___  And can I have tomato soup with bread?

**5**  48▷ **Listen and repeat the sentences in 4.**

**6**  **Work in groups of three. Practise a conversation in the cafeteria. Order food and drink from the menu in 1. Take turns to be A, B, and C.**
**Student A**  You work in the cafeteria.
**Student B**  You work at the company. You are with Student C.
**Student C**  You are a visitor at the company. You are with Student B.

**7**  49▷ **Listen to Mr Shimura and Mr Jarvis at lunch. Who says sentences 1–5? Tick (✓) *Mr Shimura* or *Mr Jarvis*.**

|  | Mr Shimura | Mr Jarvis |
|---|---|---|
| 1  I like steak. | ☐ | ☐ |
| 2  I don't like sushi. | ☐ | ☐ |
| 3  I like Japanese food. | ☐ | ☐ |
| 4  Do you like Indian food? | ☐ | ☐ |
| 5  Yes, I do. | ☐ | ☐ |

>> For more exercises, go to **Practice file 6** on page 64.

**8**  **Work in groups. Discuss the questions.**
What food do you like? Do you like the food in **1**?

Do you like food from other countries? For example, do you like Indian food? Italian food? Thai food?

***Examples: A***  *What food do you like?*     ***B***  *I like steak, but I don't like fries.*
           ***A***  *Do you like Japanese food?*   ***B***  *Yes, I do. / No, I don't.*

ⓘ >> Interactive Workbook >> **Glossary**

**Tip** | *I'd like, I like*
Say *I'd like …* when you order food:
  ***I'd like*** *chicken curry.*
Say *I like …* about food in general:
  ***I like*** *salad.*

## Language at work | *can / can't*

**1** Do you have free time at lunchtime at work? What do you do?

**2** Read about the company, EE. What do 100 employees do at lunchtime?

# EE employees sing at work

EE has offices in Merthyr Tydfil in Wales. 40 employees are in the company choir. They meet at lunchtime and they sing!

**3** 50▷ Listen to a conversation. Who sings at lunchtime? The man or the woman?

**4** 50▷ Listen again. Complete with *can* or *can't*.
**A** What do you do at lunchtime?
**B** I sing in the company choir.
**A** ¹_____ you sing?
**B** Yes, I ²_____ . Do you want to come?
**A** No. I ³_____ sing.

**5** Work in pairs. Practise the conversation in **4**.

**6** 51▷ Look at the pictures. Listen and repeat.

1 play golf    2 play the guitar    3 speak English    4 play tennis    5 run a marathon    6 cook Italian food

**7** Work in pairs. Ask and answer questions about the activities in **6**.
    *Example:* **A** *Can you play golf?*
              **B** *Yes, I can. Can you play golf?*
              **A** *No, I can't.*

>> For more information and exercises, go to **Practice file 6** on page 65.

**8** Stand up. Ask three people the questions in the table. Write their name and answers.

|  | Person 1 _____ | Person 2 _____ | Person 3 _____ |
|---|---|---|---|
| What sports can you play? |  |  |  |
| What languages can you speak? |  |  |  |
| What musical instruments can you play? |  |  |  |
| What type of food can you cook? |  |  |  |

**9** Tell the class about the three people in **8**. What can they do?

*Example:* *Mario can play tennis and football. He can speak three languages – Italian, English, and Chinese. He can't play a musical instrument, but he can sing, and he can cook Italian food!*

## Practically speaking | Days and times

**1** 52▷ Listen and complete with the days of the week. Listen again and repeat.

*Wednesday   Sunday   Friday   Tuesday*

| Monday | ▷ | | ▷ | | ▷ | Thursday | ▷ | | ▷ | Saturday | ▷ | |

**2** Work in pairs. What days do you
- go to work?
- have free time?
- play sport?

**3** Read two notices at a company.
1  What day is golf? What time does it start?
2  What day is choir? What time does it start? What time does it finish?

*Play golf after work*

*On Monday at 5.00*

*Call Nashil in Human Resources (extension 221) for information*

*Sing at lunchtime on Tuesday!*

*The company choir meets 12.00–1.00 in room 31A*

*All employees welcome*

**4** 53▷ What's the time? Complete with the number. Listen, check, and repeat.

1  It's _____ o'clock.    2  It's _____ fifteen.    3  It's _____ thirty.    4  It's _____ forty-five.

>> For more exercises, go to **Practice file 6** on page 65.

**5** Work in pairs. What time do you
- start work?
- have lunch?
- finish work?

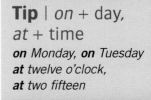

**Tip** | *on* + day, *at* + time

**on** *Monday,* **on** *Tuesday*
**at** *twelve o'clock,*
**at** *two fifteen*

## Business communication | Inviting, accepting and declining

**1** 54▷ **Listen and match the invitations to the conversations.**

*play tennis      have dinner*

Conversation 1: _____

Conversation 2: _____

**2** 54▷ **Listen again. Match 1–9 to a–i.**

| | | | |
|---|---|---|---|
| 1 | Do you like ___ | **a** | ... be nice. |
| 2 | Would you like ___ | **b** | ... Mexican food? |
| 3 | That would ___ | **c** | ... play tennis after work? |
| 4 | I'm afraid I'm ___ | **d** | ... to have dinner? |
| 5 | Is six thirty ___ | **e** | ... OK? |
| 6 | Do you want to ___ | **f** | ... I can't today. |
| 7 | I'd love to, but ___ | **g** | ... great. |
| 8 | See you ___ | **h** | ... on Thursday. |
| 9 | That'd be ___ | **i** | ... busy at six. |

**3** 55▷ **Tick (✓) the correct answer to the questions. Listen and check.**

1 Would you like to play tennis?
  **a** Yes, I'd like tennis.   **b** Yes, that'd be great.
2 Do you want to play on Friday?
  **a** I'd love to, but I can't.   **b** I'd love to, but I don't.
3 What day can you play?
  **a** Sorry, I can't.   **b** On Thursday.
4 Is six OK?
  **a** I afraid I busy at six. Is six thirty OK?
  **b** I'm afraid I'm busy at six. Is six thirty OK?

**4** **Work in pairs. Take turns. Student A, ask the four questions in 3. Student B, close your book. Answer Student A's questions.**

>> For more exercises, go to **Practice file 6** on page 64.

**5** **Work in pairs. Practise two conversations using the flowchart. Invite the other person to**
  • have dinner at a Mexican restaurant at 6.30
  • play tennis after work.

**6** **Work in pairs. Invite your partner to do something after this lesson.**

*ⓘ* >> Interactive Workbook >> **Email** and **Exercises and Tests**

## Key expressions

**Inviting**
Would you like to have dinner?
Do you want to play tennis after work?

**Accepting (saying 'Yes')**
Yes, please. That would be nice.
That'd be great. Thanks.
See you on Thursday / at seven / in reception.

**Declining (saying 'No')**
I'd love to, but I can't (today).
I'm afraid I'm busy (at six).

**Saying a day / time**
What day can you play?
What time?
Is six thirty OK?

*ⓘ* >> Interactive Workbook
  >> **Phrasebank**

## Making conversation in the restaurant

**Play the game in groups of three or four. You are in a restaurant with new clients.**

- All players go to START.
- Toss a coin.

  Heads = Move 1 square.

  Tails = Move 2 squares.
- On a blue square, follow the instructions. Talk to the person on your left.
- On a yellow square, ask the person on your right.

| START | INTRODUCE YOURSELF | What food do you like? | Do you like Italian food? | ORDER FOOD |

**FINISH**

SAY GOODBYE

Can you cook?

What languages can you speak?

What can you cook?

What sports can you play?

What musical instruments can you play?

| INVITE THE OTHER PERSON TO PLAY TENNIS ON FRIDAY | Can you play tennis? | What sports do you like? | INVITE THE OTHER PERSON TO CHOIR ON TUESDAY | Can you sing? |

Activity

# 7 | Technology

**Learning objectives in this unit**
- Talking about office technology
- Talking about what's in your office
- Giving instructions

**Activity**
- Guess the technology

## Starting point

1 **Where do you normally work (e.g. in an office, at home)?**

2 **What technology do you use?**

## Working with words | Office technology

1 56▷ **Listen and read about three people at work. Who**

1 works in Sales? _____

2 is an engineer? _____

3 is a graphic designer? _____

### Mustafa QATAR

I'm an engineer. I work for an oil company and I manage projects all over the country. In my office, I have a PC and a **printer**. On site, I have a **tablet** for notes and a **digital camera**.

### Julie AUSTRALIA

I'm a graphic designer in Brisbane, Australia and I work at home. I design websites on my laptop. I have Skype meetings with clients so I need a **webcam** and **headset**. I also have a **smartphone**, of course!

### Andrea THE NETHERLANDS

I'm in Sales. I work in an office. Sometimes I travel, and I work in my hotel room or in my car. I have a **desktop computer** in my office. When I travel, I have my **laptop** and a small **projector** with me for presentations. Oh, and my **USB stick**.

2 **Match the words in bold in 1 to the pictures.**

1 _____

2 _____

3 _____

4 _____

5 _____

6 _____

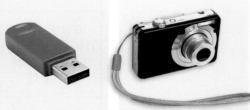

7 _____

8 _____

9 _____

10 _____

**3** 57▷ **Listen, check, and repeat.**

**4** **Work in pairs. What things in 2 do you have at work?**

**5** **Read the emails from the people in 1 and answer the questions.**

1 What is the email about? Write *Site report*, *Presentation*, or *Company logo* on the 'Subject' line.

2 Who writes the email? Write *Andrea*, *Julie*, or *Mustafa*.

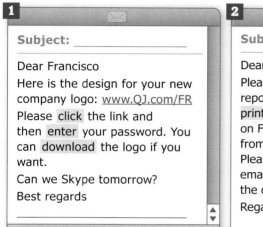

**1**

Subject: _____

Dear Francisco
Here is the design for your new company logo: www.QJ.com/FR
Please click the link and then enter your password. You can download the logo if you want.
Can we Skype tomorrow?
Best regards
_____

**2**

Subject: _____

Dear Sara
Please find attached my site report and photos. Can you print the report for the meeting on Friday? There is a document from head office on my desk. Please scan the document and email it to me. I am back in the office on Thursday.
Regards
_____

**3**

Subject: _____

Hi Laura
I am late and the sales presentation about the new product starts at 2.00 – in meeting room 1. The presentation is on my computer. Can you save it on a USB stick? And can you switch on my laptop and then connect the projector to the laptop? They're in the meeting room.
Thanks
_____

**6** **Match the highlighted verbs in 5 to the pictures.**

1 _____
  on a USB stick

2 _____
  a projector

Subject: Website
Hi Gemma,
This is the link:
www.globalinfo.co.uk

3 _____
  a link

Downloading 25% of Logo.JPEG.

4 _____
  a file

5 _____
  a document

6 _____
  a report

FTP SHARE
Username : BerniDownes
Password :
Forgot your password
Log-in

7 _____
  a password

8 _____
  to the laptop

➤➤ For more exercises, go to **Practice file 7** on page 66.

**7** **Work in pairs. Talk about the things you do / don't do at work.**
   ***Example:*** *I download information. I scan documents. I don't save documents on a USB stick.*

ⓘ ➤➤ Interactive Workbook ➤➤ Glossary

**Tip** | *computer / USB stick*

*desktop computer = PC*
*USB stick = memory stick = flash drive*

# Language at work | Possessive adjectives

**1** 58▷ **Felipe Gonzales has a new job at IUG. Listen to the conversation. Are the sentences true (*T*) or false (*F*)?**

1 Felipe is the new marketing manager. ___
2 There are six people in the team. ___
3 Nadine manages the website. ___
4 Olivier and Sandra are in the office today. ___
5 Felipe has a printer on his desk. ___

**2** 58▷ **Listen again. Match 1–7 to a–g.**

1 I'm the new marketing assistant. ___
2 We have six people in the team. ___
3 He manages key accounts. ___
4 She manages the website. ___
5 You are in this office. ___
6 They are at a conference. ___
7 The printer is here. We all use it. ___

a Her office is there.
b Your desk is here.
c My name's Felipe Gonzales.
d Their desks are over there.
e Its 'on' switch is there.
f Our project manager is Pierre.
g His office is there.

**3 Complete with the possessive adjectives from a–g in 2.**

| | Possessive adjectives | | | Possessive adjectives |
|---|---|---|---|---|
| I | my | | it | |
| you | | | we | |
| he | | | they | |
| she | | | | |

**4 Complete with possessive adjectives.**

1 I'm the Production Manager. ___*My*___ name's Antonio.
2 Selma and Luis are from Brazil, but _____ company is American.
3 He's my manager. _____ office is over there.
4 The company is German. _____ head office is in Berlin.
5 We're Marc and Rosa. This is _____ department.
6 She's from China. _____ company is Chinese.
7 You are the assistant. _____ office is here.

**5** 59▷ **Listen and read. Where is the laptop?**

A I can't find my laptop.
B Is it on your desk?
A No, it isn't.
B Is it on Pierre's desk?
A No.
B Is it in Remi and Ludo's office?
A No, it isn't there.
B Is it in your manager's office?
A Oh, yes, it is! Thanks.

**6** 59▷ **Listen again. Circle** *'s***.**

>> For more information and exercises, go to **Practice file 7** on page 67.

**Tip** | *'s*

*Pierre's desk = the desk of Pierre*
*Remi and Ludo's office = the office of Remi and Ludo*

**7** Work in pairs. Where are your things? Student A, see below. Student B, turn to File 08 on page 71.

**Student A**

1 Choose an object for each name and place.

*smartphone    USB stick    projector    laptop*

Juliette's desk _____

Andrey's office _____

the manager's desk _____

Medhat and Sultan's office _____

2 Answer Student B's questions about each object.

**Example: B** *Is my smartphone on Juliette's desk?*
  **A** *No, it isn't on her desk.*
  **B** *Is it in Medhat and Sultan's office?*
  **A** *Yes, it is in their office.*

3 Ask Student B about these objects. Match to the names and places.

*webcam    digital camera    printer    tablet*

Juliette / desk _____

Andrey / office _____

the manager / desk _____

Medhat and Sultan / office _____

## Practically speaking | *this, that, these, those*

**1** Match the sentences to the pictures. Write the letter.

1 This is my USB stick. ___

2 That's your USB stick. ___

3 Those are your documents. ___

4 These are my documents. ___

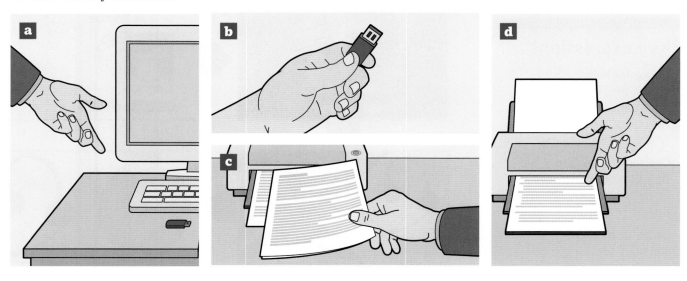

▶▶ For more exercises, go to **Practice file 7** on page 67.

**2** Work in pairs. Put three objects from your bag on the table. Talk about your objects and your partner's objects.

**Examples:** *This is (your mobile). That's (my pen).*
    *These are my (keys). Those are your (pens).*

## Business communication | Giving instructions

**1** What technology do you need for a video conference?

**2** Ryan Mitchell works for a company in Melbourne, Australia. His company works with Julie, a graphic designer in Brisbane. Normally, Ryan and Julie talk by phone. Today, they need a video conference on the computer. Ryan asks his colleague Amanda for help.

**60▷ Listen to the conversation. What technology do Ryan and Amanda talk about?**

**3** 60▷ Listen again. Match the questions to the responses.

1 What's the problem? ___
2 How does it work? ___
3 Do you have a headset? ___
4 Does it work now? ___
5 Is your microphone on? ___
6 Where do I switch it on? ___

a No, I don't.
b I don't know how to use this software.
c First, you need to enter her name.
d Yes, I think so.
e Just there.
f I don't know.

**4** Work in pairs. Practise the conversation between Ryan and Amanda. Look at the pictures. Use the questions and answers in **3** to help.

*First you need to enter her name.*

▶▶ For more exercises, go to **Practice file 7** on page 66.

**5** Work in pairs. Practise asking about technology and giving instructions. Student A, turn to File 04 on page 70. Student B, turn to File 10 on page 71.

ⓘ ▶▶ Interactive Workbook ▶▶ **Email** and **Exercises and Tests**

---

## Key expressions

**Asking for help**
What's the problem?
I don't know how to use …
How does it work?
Where do I switch it on?

**Checking equipment**
Do you have a …?
Is the … on?
Does it work now?

**Giving instructions**
You need to …

**Sequencing the instructions**
First …
Next …
Then …

ⓘ ▶▶ Interactive Workbook ▶▶ **Phrasebank**

# Guess the technology

**Work in groups of four. You are in two teams: Team A and Team B (two students in each team).**

1 Team A starts. Choose a picture. Say how the technology works. DO NOT say the name. Team B guesses the technology.

*Example:* **A** *First, you switch it on. You also need a computer. Then connect it to your computer. Next, play your music and listen.*

  **B** *It's the speaker.*

  **A** *Correct. You win a point!*

2 Team B – Your go! Repeat the activity.

3 Repeat the activity for all 16 pictures. There are 8 pictures for each team. Do not use the same picture twice.

**Your team can win 8 points. Which team is the winner?**

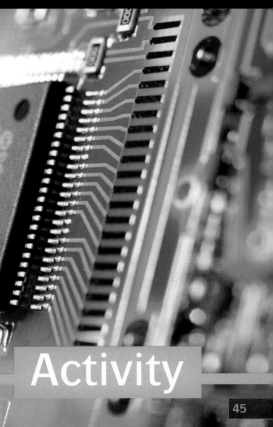

Activity

# 8 | Travel

## Learning objectives in this unit
- Talking about transport and travel
- Talking about the past
- Saying months and dates
- Arranging a meeting

## Activity
- When can we meet?

## Starting point

**1** What time do you
- leave for work?
- arrive at work?

**How long does it take?**

**2** Do you travel for your job? Where do you travel?

## Working with words | Transport and travel

**1** Read the pie chart about travel in Japan. Answer the questions.
1 What percentage (%) of people go to work by car?
2 What percentage of people walk to work?
3 What percentage of people go to work by train?

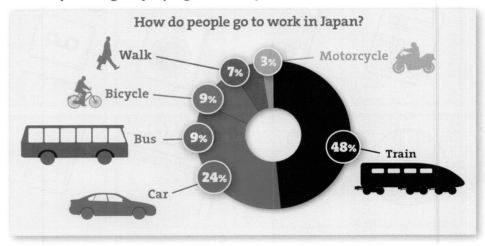

How do people go to work in Japan?

Walk — 7%
Motorcycle — 3%
Bicycle — 9%
Bus — 9%
Train — 48%
Car — 24%

**2** 61▷ Listen and repeat the transport words.

●    ●    ●    ●••    ●•• ••
car    bus    train    bicycle    motorcycle

**3** Find out about your class. Ask people the question and tick (✓) the answers.
*Example: A How do you go to work?*    *B I walk.*

| How do you go to work? | Answers |
| --- | --- |
| I walk. | ✓ |
| I go by car. | |
| I go by train. | |
| I go by bus. | |
| I go by bicycle. | |
| I go by motorcycle. | |
| Other? (Write answers) | |

## Tip | go, travel
Use *go* for everyday travel:
*I **go** to work by train.*
Use *travel* for long journeys:
*I **travel** from London to Sydney.*

**4** Work in pairs. Draw a pie chart for the answers in **3**. Present the chart to your class.

> *Example: Five people walk to work. / 25 per cent of the class walk to work.*

**5** 62▷ Donald Jones is on a business trip. Listen to two conversations and tick (✓) the transport.

taxi ☐    bus ☐    train ☐    plane ☐

**6** Find the things in the pictures. Write the letter.

terminal ___    bag ___    passport ___

receipt ___    boarding gate ___    e-ticket ___

**7** Complete with the verbs.

> *want (x2)    take    check in    leave    go    arrive    have*

1 Can you _____ me to the airport?

2 Which terminal do you _____?

3 Do you _____ a receipt?

4 Can I _____ your passport and e-ticket, please?

5 Do you have any bags to _____?

6 Your flight _____s at one o'clock.

7 Please _____ to the boarding gate at twelve fifteen.

8 What time does the flight _____ in Muscat?

**8** 62▷ Listen again and check.

>> For more exercises, go to **Practice file 8** on page 68.

**9** Work in pairs. Practise Donald's two conversations.

| | |
|---|---|
| **1 In the taxi**<br>**A** Ask for the airport.<br>**B** Ask which terminal.<br>**A** Reply.<br>**B** Say the price. Ask about receipt.<br>**A** Reply. | **2 At the airport**<br>**A** Say your flight.<br>**B** Ask for passport, ticket, and bags.<br>**A** Reply.<br>**B** Give boarding card. / Say when flight leaves.<br>**A** Ask when flight arrives.<br>**B** Say the time. |

ⓘ >> Interactive Workbook >> Glossary

**Tip** | *take + transport*

*take* + transport = travel by transport:

**take a taxi** to the airport

## Language at work | *was / were*

**1** 63▷ Donald Jones is in his office. Alice asks about his business trip. Match the words to the time phrases.

| | | | |
|---|---|---|---|
| 1 | Dubai | ___ | **a** last Wednesday and Thursday |
| 2 | Oman and the UAE | ___ | **b** yesterday |
| 3 | Muscat | ___ | **c** last week |
| 4 | on holiday | ___ | **d** for five days |

**2** 63▷ Listen to the conversation again. <u>Underline</u> *was, were, wasn't,* or *weren't*.

**Alice**   Hi, Donald. Where were you yesterday?

**Donald**   In Dubai. I ¹*was / were* in Oman and the UAE for five days.

**Alice**   Oh, yes. How ²*was / were* your trip?

**Donald**   OK. Our clients in Muscat ³*was / were* very happy with the new machines.

**Alice**   Great! Was Muscat nice?

**Donald**   I don't know, because I ⁴*wasn't / weren't* there very long. Er … I was in Muscat last Wednesday and Thursday and then there ⁵*was / were* two meetings in Dubai yesterday. But they ⁶*wasn't / weren't* very useful. And what about you? ⁷*Was / Were* you busy last week?

**Alice**   I ⁸*wasn't / weren't* here. I was on holiday.

**3** Complete the rules for the verb *be* with *am / is / are* or *was / were*.

We talk about the present with _____ .

We talk about the past with _____ .

**4** Read the next part of the conversation. Complete with *was, were, wasn't,* or *weren't*.

**Donald**   How ¹_____ your holiday?

**Alice**   Great. We ²_____ in Barcelona for six days.

**Donald**   I was in Barcelona last year. It was a sales conference, so it ³_____ a holiday. The restaurants ⁴_____ very good, but the city ⁵_____ busy. Were there hundreds of tourists?

**Alice**   No, there ⁶_____ . It was quiet in the centre.

**5** 64▷ Listen and check.

**6** Work in pairs. Last week Donald and Alice were on a business trip. Look at the pictures. Say sentences about the trip.

*Example: They were in Paris last Monday …*

| Monday and Tuesday | Wednesday | Thursday and Friday |
|---|---|---|

**7** **Work in pairs. Ask and answer questions.**

Where were you

- yesterday?   • last night?   • last weekend?

>> For more information and exercises, go to **Practice file 8** on page 69.

**8** **Work in pairs. Ask questions about two business trips. Student A, turn to File 05 on page 70. Student B, turn to File 11 on page 72.**

## Practically speaking | Months and dates

**1** **65▷ Listen and repeat the months.**

| January | February | March | April | May | June |
| July | August | September | October | November | December |

**2** **66▷ Listen to the conversation. Tick (✓) the months in 1 you hear.**

**3** **66▷ Listen again. Mark (✗) the dates of these events.**

*last trip to Turin    next trip    factory visit    sales conference*

### JUNE

| M | Tu | W | Th | F | Sa | Su |
|---|---|---|---|---|---|---|
| 1 | 2 | 3 | 4 | 5 | 6 | 7 |
| 8 | 9 | 10 | 11 | 12 | 13 | 14 |
| 15 | 16 | 17 | 18 | 19 | 20 | 21 |
| 22 | 23 | 24 | 25 | 26 | 27 | 28 |
| 29 | 30 | | | | | |

### JULY

| M | Tu | W | Th | F | Sa | Su |
|---|---|---|---|---|---|---|
| | | 1 | 2 | 3 | 4 | 5 |
| 6 | 7 | 8 | 9 | 10 | 11 | 12 |
| 13 | 14 | 15 | 16 | 17 | 18 | 19 |
| 20 | 21 | 22 | 23 | 24 | 25 | 26 |
| 27 | 28 | 29 | 30 | 31 | | |

### AUGUST

| M | Tu | W | Th | F | Sa | Su |
|---|---|---|---|---|---|---|
| 31 | | | | | 1 | 2 |
| 3 | 4 | 5 | 6 | 7 | 8 | 9 |
| 10 | 11 | 12 | 13 | 14 | 15 | 16 |
| 17 | 18 | 19 | 20 | 21 | 22 | 23 |
| 24 | 25 | 26 | 27 | 28 | 29 | 30 |

### SEPTEMBER

| M | Tu | W | Th | F | Sa | Su |
|---|---|---|---|---|---|---|
| | 1 | 2 | 3 | 4 | 5 | 6 |
| 7 | 8 | 9 | 10 | 11 | 12 | 13 |
| 14 | 15 | 16 | 17 | 18 | 19 | 20 |
| 21 | 22 | 23 | 24 | 25 | 26 | 27 |
| 28 | 29 | 30 | | | | |

### OCTOBER

| M | Tu | W | Th | F | Sa | Su |
|---|---|---|---|---|---|---|
| | | 1 | 2 | 3 | 4 |
| 5 | 6 | 7 | 8 | 9 | 10 | 11 |
| 12 | 13 | 14 | 15 | 16 | 17 | 18 |
| 19 | 20 | 21 | 22 | 23 | 24 | 25 |
| 26 | 27 | 28 | 29 | 30 | 31 | |

### NOVEMBER

| M | Tu | W | Th | F | Sa | Su |
|---|---|---|---|---|---|---|
| 30 | | | | | | 1 |
| 2 | 3 | 4 | 5 | 6 | 7 | 8 |
| 9 | 10 | 11 | 12 | 13 | 14 | 15 |
| 16 | 17 | 18 | 19 | 20 | 21 | 22 |
| 23 | 24 | 25 | 26 | 27 | 28 | 29 |

**4** **67▷ Listen and repeat the dates.**

| 1st June | 3rd August | 14th August |
| 11th September | 27th November | 30th November |

>> For more exercises, go to **Practice file 8** on page 69.

**5** **Work in pairs. Ask and answer the questions.**

What's the date today?
When's your birthday?
When was your last holiday?

**Tip | Saying the date**

We say:
*the eighteenth of March*
We write:
*18th March*
*18 March*
*18/3*

## Business communication | Arranging a meeting

**1** **Read the email from Simon about a meeting. Answer the questions.**

1  When is the meeting?       2  What is the meeting about?

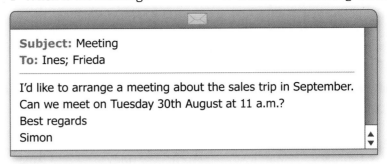

**Subject:** Meeting
**To:** Ines; Frieda

I'd like to arrange a meeting about the sales trip in September.
Can we meet on Tuesday 30th August at 11 a.m.?
Best regards
Simon

**2** **Read the replies. Answer the questions.**

1  Who can go to the meeting?       2  Who can't go? Why not?

Dear Simon
I'm sorry, I can't meet on Tuesday
30th August. I'm visiting our factory.
Kind regards
Ines

Hi Simon
Tuesday 30th August is fine for me.
See you at 11 a.m.
Regards
Frieda

**3** **68▷ Simon calls Ines. Listen to the conversation. When can they meet?**

**4** **68▷ Listen again. Complete with the words.**

| I'm busy | Are you free | Can we arrange | How about |
|---|---|---|---|
| What time | I'm free | Is … OK | |

**Simon**  It's about the meeting. ¹_____ a new date and time?

**Ines**  Yes, of course.

**Simon**  ²_____ on Wednesday 31st at 2 p.m.?

**Ines**  Sorry, ³_____. I'm visiting the factory on Tuesday and Wednesday.

**Simon**  ⁴_____ Thursday morning? Are you free then?

**Ines**  Yes, ⁵_____ on Thursday morning. ⁶_____ is good for you?

**Simon**  ⁷_____ 10 a.m. _____ for you?

**5** **69▷ Match 1–6 to a–f. Then listen and check.**

1  I'd like to arrange ___          a  … on Tuesday 3rd April.
2  I'm free ___                     b  … I'm busy.
3  Is 2 p.m. ___                    c  … a meeting.
4  How about ___                    d  … OK for you?
5  Sorry, ___                       e  … is fine for me.
6  The 21st April ___               f  … Friday 11th February?

**》** For more exercises, go to **Practice file 8** on page 68.

**6** **Work in pairs. Student A, turn to File 02 on page 70. Student B, turn to File 14 on page 72.**

---

ⓘ **》** Interactive Workbook **》 Email** and **Exercises and Tests**

---

## Key expressions

**Arranging to meet**
I'd like to arrange a meeting.
Can we arrange a new date and time?

**Asking about dates and times**
How about (Wednesday)?
Can we meet on / at …?
Are you free on (Monday) / at (2 p.m.)?
What time is good for you?
Is (9 a.m.) OK for you?

**Saying you are free**
I'm free on (Friday) / at (3 p.m.).
(Tuesday) is fine for me.

**Saying you are not free**
Sorry, I'm busy.
I'm sorry, I can't meet on (30th June) / at (11 a.m.).

ⓘ **》** Interactive Workbook
**》 Phrasebank**

# When can we meet?

Work in groups of four. Divide your group into Pair A and Pair B. Pair A, see below. Pair B, turn to File 13 on page 72.

## Pair A

**1** Read information 1–3. Complete your calendar below.

1
### KLM FLIGHT SÃO PAULO – FRANKFURT
DATE: 18TH APRIL
FLIGHT TIME: 12.00
RETURN FLIGHT: 23RD APRIL

2
**TDI Annual Sales Conference**
Frankfurt | 20th–22nd April

**Tdi**

3
**Subject:** Sales trip
**To:** Gerard, Igor

This is to confirm your sales trip to Hungary.
The dates for your calendar are 8th–11th May.
Best
Ricardo

## April–May

| 15 | 16 | 17 | 18 | 19 | 20 | 21 |
| 22 | 23 | 24 | 25 Holiday | 26 | 27 | 28 |
| 29 | 30 | 1 May | 2 | 3 | 4 | 5 |
| 6 | 7 | 8 | 9 | 10 | 11 | 12 |

**2** 70▷ Listen to a voicemail message. Write the information in your calendar.

**3** Have a teleconference with Pair B. Arrange a date for a meeting.

**Activity**

51

# The revision game

**Work in pairs. Take turns to choose a square.**

Talk to your partner.

Read the instruction and answer.

Answer the questions.

**Complete and win five squares in a row, across (→), down (↓), or diagonally (↘).**

---

Introduce yourself.

Correct the mistake.

*Are you Maria?*
*Yes, I are.*

Ask and answer three questions about your company.

You have a plane journey. Say three things you need.

Call your partner.
**You:** Ask for Piotr.
**Partner:** Say he's out. Take a message.

How many people work in your …
– department?
– company?

Say five transport words.

Call your partner.
**You:** Order two boxes of paper.
**Partner:** Take the order.

What's your company? Can you spell it?

You are in a café.
**You:** Order lunch.
**Partner:** Take the order.

Ask and answer about your last business trip or holiday:

*How was it?*

Say two sentences about your company or department with:

*There is …*
*There are …*

What's your favourite …
- food?
- type of restaurant?

☐

Say three jobs in your company.

☐

Where were you last Monday?

☐

Call your partner.
**You:** Ask for Rosa.
**Partner:** Say she's out. Take a message.

☐

What day was yesterday?

What is the first day of the week?

☐

Say three departments in your company.

☐

Ask and answer three questions about your work.

**Example:** *Do you work in a team?*

☐

Correct the mistake.
*Please find attach the map.*

☐

Does your company sell or make products?
What does it sell or make?

☐

Say three sentences about what you do at work.

☐

Where are you now?
Are you in your office?

☐

Say three countries and three nationalities.

**Example:**
*the UK ➔ British*

☐

Are you from Spain?
Where's your head office?

☐

Invite your partner somewhere.
Arrange to meet.

☐

Say three abilities.

**Example:** *I can use PowerPoint software.*

☐

Call your partner.
Arrange a date and time for a sales meeting.

☐

Say three adjectives about your workplace and company buildings.

☐

Say goodbye to your partner.

☐

53

## Working with words

**1 Complete with the words.**

~~Hello~~  I'm  my name  Hi

A ¹_____Hello_____ , ²_____'s Monika Kelly.

B ³_____ , ⁴_____ Laurie.

**2 Match the questions to the answers.**

1 What's your name? ____   a I'm a manager.

2 What's your job? ____   b I'm Katja.

**3 Look at the pictures. Complete the jobs.**

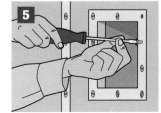

1 IT t __ __ __ __ __ __ __ __ n

2 f __ __ __ __ __ e director

3 office a __ __ __ __ __ __ __ __ t

4 human resources m __ __ __ __ __ r

5 e __ __ __ __ __ __ r

6 sales r __ __ __ __ __ __ __ __ __ __ __ __ __ e

**4 Complete with *a* or *an*.**

1 _____a_____ manager

2 _____an_____ assistant

3 _____ IT technician

4 _____ technician

5 _____ director

6 _____ office manager

7 _____ engineer

8 _____ sales representative

**5 Read the name badges. Complete the conversations with *a / an* + job.**

> **Arnaud Cagnol**
> Engineer

> **Lance Jones**
> IT Technician

A What's your job, Arnaud?

B I'm ¹_____. And you?

A I'm ²_____.

> **Ahmed Al Omran**
> Finance Director

> **Josh Armstrong**
> Sales Representative

A My name's Josh Armstrong. I'm ³_____.
What's your job?

B I'm ⁴_____.

## Business communication

**1 Put the conversations in the right order.**

1 a ____ Nice to meet you, Zoran. I'm Xavier.

  b __1__ Good morning. Are you Zoran?

  c ____ Yes, I am.

2 a ____ I'm Abi and this is Kashyar.

  b ____ Nice to meet you too.

  c ____ Nice to meet you, Kashyar.

3 a ____ Nice to meet you too, Zoran. Goodbye.

  b ____ Yes, see you soon, Xavier. And it was nice meeting you, Kasyar.

  c ____ See you soon, Zoran.

**2 Underline the correct word(s) in *italics*.**

A ¹*Hello / Good* afternoon. What's your name?

B ²*My name / I'm* Alek.

A What's your ³*first name / surname*?

B It's Sagarra.

A ⁴*What's / Are* you Petra?

C Yes, I am.

A I'm Laura and ⁵*this is / this is my* Alek Sagarra.

C Nice to meet you, Alek.

B Nice to meet you ⁶*too / soon*.

A ⁷*Goodbye / See you* soon, Alek.

B Goodbye, Laura. And it was nice ⁸*meet / meeting* you too, Petra.

C Yes, bye.

## Practically speaking

**Write in the letters with the same sound.**

E  U  K  T  N  X  Y

A  H  J  <sup>1</sup>___
B  C  D  <sup>2</sup>___  G  P  <sup>3</sup>___  V
F  L  M  <sup>4</sup>___  S  <sup>5</sup>___  Z
I  <sup>6</sup>___
O
Q  <sup>7</sup>___  W
R

## Language at work | I'm / you're / Are you ...?

*To be*

**Form**

**Positive:**

| I | 'm | Alex. |
|---|---|---|
| I | am | Monika. |
| You | 're | a technician. |
| You | are | a director. |

**Negative:**

| I | 'm not | an assistant. |
|---|---|---|
| I | am not | a manager. |
| You | 're not | an engineer. |
| You | are not | a technician. |

**Questions:**

| Am | I | a manager? |
|---|---|---|
| Are | you | Laura? |

**Short answers:**

| Yes, | I | am. |
|---|---|---|
| | you | are. |
| No, | I | 'm not. |
| | you | aren't. |

A *Are you a director?*
B *Yes, I am. I'm a finance director.*
A *Are you a manager?*
B *No, I'm not. I'm an assistant.*
A *You're a manager.*
B *No, I'm not. I'm a director.*
A *You're not a technician.*
B *Yes, I am.*

**1** Underline the correct verb in *italics*.

1 Hello, I *'m / 're* Isadora.
2 And you *am / are* Alek.
3 No, I *'m / 're* not. I'm Alex.
4 You *am not / are not* an engineer. You're a technician.

**2** Complete with *'m, 're, 'm not,* or *'re not.*

1 You _____ a manager.
2 No, I _____ a manager.
3 I _____ a director.
4 You _____ a director. You're a manager.

**3** Underline the correct verb in *italics*.

A Are you an assistant?
B Yes, I <sup>1</sup>*'m / am.* I'm an office assistant.
A <sup>2</sup>*Am / Are* you an assistant?
C No, I <sup>3</sup>*'m not / not.* I'm a manager.

**4** Complete with the correct verbs.

A <sup>1</sup>_____ you Tomas?
B Yes, I <sup>2</sup>_____. Are you Enid?
A No, I <sup>3</sup>_____. I'm Laura.

**5** Tick (✓) the correct sentence, a or b.

1 a Hi. I'm Kashyar.
  b Hi. I're Kashyar.
2 a Am you Maria?
  b Are you Maria?
3 a Your Rachel.
  b You're Rachel.
4 a You're not an engineer.
  b You am not an engineer.
5 Are you a manager?
  a Yes, I'm.
  b Yes, I am.
6 Are you Xavier?
  a No, I'm not. I'm Alex.
  b No, I not. I Alex.

## Working with words

**1 Complete with the words.**

company   South Korea   office   Samsung

**A** Hi, I work for [1]_____ in [2]_____ _____ .

**B** My [3]_____ is BMW. The head [4]_____ is in Munich.

**2 Complete the country names with *a, e, i, o,* or *u*.**

1  B r __ z __ l
2  S __ __ d __   __ r __ b __ __
3  J __ p __ n
4  G __ r m __ n y
5  S __ __ t h   K __ r __ __
6  C h __ n __
7  S p __ __ n
8  K __ w __ __ t

**3 Look at the business cards. Complete the information.**

**Taro Nakamura**
Engineer
Honda, Tokyo, Japan

1  My name's _____ . I'm from _____ .
My company is _____ . The head office is in _____ .

**Jenny Thomas**
Sales Manager
Nike Inc
Oregon
USA

2  I'm _____ . I'm from _____ .
I work for _____ . The head office is in _____ .

**Robert Bosisio**
IT Technician
Inditex
Arteixo | Spain

3  My name's _____ . I'm from _____ .
My company is _____ . The head office is in _____ .

**4 Put the words in the right order.**

1  you / from / Where / are
_____?

2  office / is / Where / your / head
_____?

3  your / company / What / is
_____?

**5 Match the questions in 4 to the answers.**

**a**  My company is Siemens. ___
**b**  It's in Zurich. ___
**c**  I'm from Brazil. ___

## Business communication

**1 Put the conversations in the right order.**

1  **a**  ___ Yes, of course. One moment.
   **b**  ___ Good afternoon. Can I speak to Regis, please?
   **c**  ___ Thanks.
   **d**  *1* Good afternoon. IP Electronics.

2  **a**  ___ No, I'm sorry, she's not in the office.
   **b**  ___ Good morning, Pascale speaking.
   **c**  ___ OK. Thanks.
   **d**  ___ Hello, Is Simone there?

**2 Complete the conversations with the words.**

speaking   there   One moment

**A** Hello, Sara [1]_____ .
**B** Hi. Is Loic [2]_____ ?
**A** Yes, sure. [3]_____ .
**B** Thanks.

that   It's   in the office   out

**A** Hi, Is [4]_____ Pauline?
**B** No, it isn't. [5]_____ Gemma.
**A** Is Pauline [6]_____ ?
**B** No, I'm sorry. She's [7]_____ .
**A** OK. Thanks.

**3 Underline the correct word(s) in *italics*.**

**A** Good morning, Cisco Systems.
**B** Hello. Can I [1]*speak / speaking* to Hugo, please?
**A** Yes, [2]*it is / of course*. [3]*A / One* moment.
**B** [4]*OK, thanks / No, thanks*.

## Practically speaking

**Match 1–4 to a–d.**

1  My phone number is 07700819527. ____
2  Flight KLM 214 is ready for boarding. ____
3  The security code is 2424. ____
4  My passport number is 017317589. ____

a  two four two four
b  zero one seven three one seven five eight nine
c  zero seven seven zero zero eight one nine five two seven
d  two one four

## Language at work | *is / isn't*

### To be

**Form**

**Positive:**

| He / She / It | is | in the head office. |
|---|---|---|
| He / She / It | 's | in Frankfurt. |

**Negative:**

| He / She / It | is not | in Chile. |
|---|---|---|
| He / She / It | isn't | in Japan. |

**Questions:**

| Is | he / she / it | in Brazil? |
|---|---|---|

**Short answers:**

| Yes, | he / she / it | is. |
|---|---|---|
| No, | he / she / it | isn't. |

*Richard **is** in the Recife office.*

*She's in China.*

*It **isn't** in Spain.*

*A  **Is** he in Saudi Arabia?*

*B  Yes, he **is**.*

*A  **Is** the head office in São Paulo?*

*B  No, it **isn't**. It's in Rio.*

**1  Complete with *is* (*'s*) or *isn't*.**

1  Paul's in China. He _____ in Japan.
2  Clara isn't in Germany. She _____ in Spain.
3  The head office is in Milan. It _____ in Rome.
4  He isn't in Brazil. He _____ in the USA.
5  The company isn't in Saudi Arabia. It _____ in Kuwait.
6  She's in Tokyo. She _____ in Seoul.

**2  Match the questions to the answers.**

1  Is Henri in China? ____
2  Is Carole in the Rome office? ____
3  Is your company ING? ____

a  No, it isn't. It's ICI.
b  Yes, he is. He's in Beijing.
c  No, she isn't. She's in the Milan office.

**3  Tick (✓) the correct sentence, a or b.**

1  a  He not in Kuwait.
   b  He isn't in Kuwait.
2  a  My company is Electrolux.
   b  My company Electrolux.
3  a  Is she's in the head office?
   b  Is she in the head office?
4  a  Yes, it in Japan.
   b  Yes, it's in Japan.
5  a  She's from Spain.
   b  She from Spain.
6  a  Is it's in Berlin?
   b  Is it in Berlin?

**4  Complete with the correct verbs.**

A  [1]_____ your company in South Korea?
B  Yes, it [2]_____. And your company?
A  It [3]_____ in South Korea. It [4]_____ in Japan.

A  [5]_____ Regis in the Rio office?
B  No, he [6]_____. He [7]_____ in the São Paulo office.

A  Sara [8]_____ in Germany. She [9]_____ in Italy.
B  [10]_____ she in Rome?
A  No, she [11]_____. She [12]_____ in Turin.

# 3 | Practice file

## Working with words

**1** Look at the pictures. Find the places in the box.

| r | e | c | e | p | t | i | o | n |
|---|---|---|---|---|---|---|---|---|
| e | c | a | r | p | a | r | k | o |
| c | a | f | z | a | f | l | t | f |
| d | y | e | o | t | a | o | a | f |
| e | m | t | t | u | c | d | x | i |
| h | n | e | o | f | t | t | o | c |
| w | a | r | e | h | o | u | s | e |
| o | r | i | a | w | r | e | c | e |
| n | f | a | c | t | y | w | h | i |

**2** Match the opposite adjectives.

1 new ___      **a** small
2 big ___      **b** bad
3 good ___     **c** old

**3** Rewrite the sentences.

1 The office is new.       It's ___*a new office*___.
2 The factory is old.      It's _____.
3 The cafeteria is good.   It's _____.
4 The car park is big.     It's _____.
5 The warehouse is small.  It's _____.

## Business communication

**1** Complete the words.

> Hi Adira
>
> ¹T __ __ __ __ s for your email. ²H __ __ __ is a map of my company. ³P __ __ __ __ __ send me a map of your company.
>
> ⁴A __ __ the best
>
> Heiner

**2** <u>Underline</u> the correct word(s) in *italics*.

> ¹ *Dear / Hello* Mr Chen
>
> ² *I write / I'm writing* about my visit to your head office. ³ *Are you / Can you* send me the address?
>
> ⁴ *Best / Kind* wishes
>
> Kimberly Black

**3** Match 1–5 to a–e.

1 Thank you ___
2 I'm writing ___
3 Can you send ___
4 Please find ___
5 Kind ___

**a** … about my visit.
**b** … attached a map.
**c** … for your email.
**d** … regards
**e** … me your number?

**4** Complete the formal phrases.

1 Hello Madelaine          ___*Dear*___ Madelaine
2 Thanks for your          _____ _____
  email.                   for your email.
3 Please send a            _____ _____
  photograph.              please send a photograph?
4 Here is the              _____ _____
  document.                attached the document.
5 Best                     Best _____

## Practically speaking

**Read and tick (✓) the correct email or website address.**

1   www dot uk dot tata dot com
   a   www.uk.tata.com
   b   www.uktata.com
   c   www.tata.co.uk

2   paolo underscore boas at meteo dot pt
   a   paolo.boas@meteo.com
   b   paolo-boas@meteo.pt
   c   paolo_boas@meteo.pt

3   k dot steger at gp dash oil dot com
   a   k.steger@gp_oil.com
   b   k.steger@gp-oil.com
   c   k-steger@gpoil.com

## Language at work | We / They are | Wh- questions

### To be

**Form**

**Positive:**

| We / They | 're | in the office. |
|---|---|---|
| We / They | are | in the car park. |
| Sonia and Bill | are | in the factory. |

**Negative:**

| We / They | aren't | in reception. |
|---|---|---|
| We / They | are not | in the warehouse. |
| Sonia and Bill | are not | in the cafeteria. |

**Questions:**

| Are | we / they | in the warehouse? |
|---|---|---|

**Short answers:**

| Yes, | we / they | are. |
|---|---|---|
| No, | we / they | aren't. |

### Wh- questions

| What | 's | your name? |
|---|---|---|
| What | are | your jobs? |
| Where | 's | the head office? |
| Where | are | the warehouses? |
| Who | 's | your director? |
| Who | are | they? |

We **are** in the cafeteria.

A **Are** Sonia and Bill in reception?    B Yes, they **are**.
A **Are** they in the factory?    B No, they **aren't**.
A **Where are** the factories?    B They**'re** in Delhi.

---

**1   Complete with 're, are, or aren't.**

1   They aren't in the warehouse. They _____ in the factory.

2   We're in the sales office. We _____ in the head office.

3   Gail and Konrad aren't in the car park. They _____ in reception.

4   The offices are new. They _____ old offices.

5   _____ they in your office?

6   No, they _____ .

7   _____ we in your office?

8   Yes, we _____ .

**2   Correct the verb to be.**

1   I are a manager.
   _____

2   Is you an IT technician?
   _____

3   Is he from Germany?
   Yes, he are.
   _____

4   Are the offices new?
   No, they isn't.
   _____

**3   Match the questions to the answers.**

1   What's your name? ____
2   Where are you from? ____
3   Who is he? ____
4   What's your job? ____
5   Where are the new offices? ____
6   Who are they? ____

a   Sales assistant.
b   In Toronto.
c   Canada.
d   Lisa Quayle.
e   The Sales Manager and the Finance Director.
f   My manager.

**4   Complete with a question word + 's or are.**

1   Wh_____ _____ your surname?    *Jones.*
2   Wh_____ _____ you from?    *New Zealand.*
3   Wh_____ _____ your job?    *I'm an engineer.*
4   Wh_____ _____ the factories?    *In Singapore and Hong Kong.*
5   Wh_____ _____ your manager?    *Mr Clements.*

## Working with words

**1** Put the letters in the right order.

1 s l l e _____
2 m t e e _____
3 w k o r _____
4 m n g e a a _____
5 h e a v _____
6 l v i e _____

**2** Complete with the verbs from **1**.

1 I'm from France and I _____ in Paris.
2 I _____ for GSK. It's a pharmaceutical company.
3 We _____ our products all over the world.
4 We _____ factories in France, the UK, and the USA.
5 I _____ the Sales Department. I have eight people in my team.
6 The sales reps _____ customers and sell our products.

**3** Match 1–6 to a–f.

1 manage the money ___
2 meet customers and sell products ___
3 meet new employees ___
4 make the products ___
5 manage the company computers ___
6 transport the products ___

a Human Resources
b Logistics
c Production
d Finance
e IT
f Sales

**4** Write the plurals.

1 company _____
2 customer _____
3 person _____
4 office _____
5 department _____
6 country _____
7 employee _____
8 factory _____

## Business communication

**1** Who says the phrases, the caller (*C*) or the receiver (*R*)?

1 Can I take a message? ___
2 I'm calling about the new product. ___
3 Please call me back as soon as possible. ___
4 I'll give Claudia your message. ___
5 Is there anything else? ___
6 Go ahead. ___

**2** Put the conversation in the right order.

**Part 1**

a ___ Hi. Is Tomas there?
b ___ OK. Go ahead.
c _1_ Production. Hello?
d ___ No, I'm sorry, he's out. Can I take a message?
e ___ Yes, it's Sonia in Sales. I'm calling about the new product.
f ___ It's about product SM 4389X1. There's a problem.

**Part 2**

a _1_ Sorry, Can you repeat that?
b ___ OK. Is there anything else?
c ___ OK. I'll give Tomas your message.
d ___ There's a problem with SM 4389X1.
e ___ That's right.
f ___ Yes. Please call me back as soon as possible. My number is 0963 325 449.
g ___ So that's 0963 325 449.

**3** Complete the conversations with the phrases.

Can I take a message?    I'll give Claudia your message.
I'm calling about    Can you repeat that?
Please call me back as soon as possible.    So that's

1 A Good morning. Can I speak to Claudia?
  B I'm sorry, she's out.
  _____

2 A Hi, _____ the new assistants, George and Chloe.
  B Sorry, I don't understand.
  _____
  A It's about George and Chloe, the new assistants.
  B OK. Go ahead.

3 A _____ My phone number is 08762 534 212.
  B _____ 08762 534 212.
  A That's right
  B OK. _____

# Practically speaking

<u>Underline</u> the correct verb in *italics*.

1 There *'s* / *are* five people in my department.
2 There *'s* / *are* a Logistics Department.
3 There *'s* / *are* an assistant.
4 There *'s* / *are* ten offices in Europe.
5 There *'s* / *are* one project manager.
6 There *'s* / *are* seven departments.

# Language at work | Present simple: *I / you / we / they*

## Form

**Positive:**

|       |         |                          |
|-------|---------|--------------------------|
|       | live    | in Tokyo.                |
| I     | manage  | the IT Department.       |
| You   | work    | for a software company.  |
| We    | sell    | products.                |
| They  | work    | in Finance.              |
|       | meet    | people.                  |

**Negative:**

|       |             |              |
|-------|-------------|--------------|
| I     |             |              |
| You   | don't work  | in Sales.    |
| We    | don't live  | in Brazil.   |
| They  | don't make  | products.    |

**Questions:**

Do you / we / they work in Sales?
Do you / we / they live in Brazil?

**Short answers:**

Yes, I / you /we / they do.
No, I / you /we / they don't.

**Questions with question words:**

|       |    |      | work?      |
|-------|----|------|------------|
| Where |    | you  | live?      |
| What  | do | we   | sell?      |
| Who   |    | they | manage?    |
|       |    |      | work for?  |

*We **work** for GSK.*
*They **don't live** in Munich.*
*Where **do** you **live**?*
*What **do** you **do**?*
*Who **do** they **work** for?*
*A **Do** you **work** in Sales?*
*B No, I **don't**. / Yes, I **do**.*

## 1 Complete with the phrases.

don't live   They meet   I work (x2)
I manage   They don't sell   I live   We have

My name's Giorgio. ¹_____ for Siemens.
I'm from Rome, but I ²_____ in Italy.
³_____ in New York. Siemens is a global
company. ⁴_____ offices all over the world.
⁵_____ in the Human Resources
Department. ⁶_____ a team of three people.
⁷_____ products. ⁸_____
new employees in the company.

## 2 Write questions. Complete the short answers.

1 A you / live / in Japan _Do you live in Japan_?
  B Yes, I do.
2 A you / work / in Finance _____?
  B No, we _____.
3 A they / have / factories / in Germany
   _____?
  B Yes, they _____.
4 A they / manage / people _____?
  B No, they _____.

## 3 Match 1–6 to a–f.

1 Where do you live? ____
2 Who do you work for? ____
3 Do you work in Frankfurt? ____
4 What do you do? ____
5 Do they work in Sales? ____
6 Do you make products? ____

a I'm a production manager.
b Yes, they do.
c I live in China.
d No, we don't. We sell products.
e We work for Airbus.
f No, I don't. I work in Munich.

## 4 Write the questions.

1 A _____?
  B I'm an IT technician.
2 A _____?
  B We work for a big finance company.
3 A _____?
  B They live in South Korea.
4 A _____?
  B I work for Air France.
5 A _____?
  B They are sales reps.

## Working with words

**1 Match 1–5 to a–e.**

1 Carrefour is a retail company. ____
2 Boeing is an aeronautical company. ____
3 Tata Motors is an automobile company. ____
4 Shell is an energy company. ____
5 Sony is an electronics company. ____

a We make televisions.
b We make cars.
c We sell food.
d We make aeroplanes.
e We sell oil and gas.

**2 Complete with the verbs.**

have    sell    order    make

American Apparel is a clothes retail company. We ¹_____ the clothes in a big factory in Los Angeles. We ²_____ the clothes in 285 shops around the world. We ³_____ a website and customers ⁴_____ clothes from the online store.

design    build    buy

IKEA is a Swedish company. We ⁵_____ products for the home. Customers ⁶_____ the products from our shops and they ⁷_____ the products at home.

**3 Write the country or nationality.**

| | Country | Nationality |
|---|---|---|
| 1 | the USA | _____ |
| 2 | _____ | Brazilian |
| 3 | China | _____ |
| 4 | _____ | English |
| 5 | Italy | _____ |
| 6 | _____ | Indian |
| 7 | Japan | _____ |
| 8 | _____ | Mexican |

## Business communication

**1 Put the words in the right order to make questions.**

1 Can / help / you / I
_____?
2 Do / have / the / you / item / number
_____?
3 How / you / like / many / would
_____?
4 What / price / the / 's
_____?
5 Does / include / delivery / that
_____?
6 Can / by / email / my / order / you / confirm
_____?

**2 Match the questions in 1 to the answers.**

a ____ One chair is 35 euros.
b ____ Yes, it does.
c ____ Five, please.
d ____ Yes, of course. What's your email?
e ____ I'd like to order black office chairs.
f ____ Yes, it's OC-31-B.

**3 Complete with the words.**

order    have    include    confirm
email    want    like    help

A Hello, can I ¹_____ you?
B Yes, I'd like to ²_____ some boxes.
A Do you ³_____ the item number?
B No, sorry, I don't. It's the Single Wall boxes in your catalogue.
A OK. That's item SW-110. How many would you ⁴_____?
B I ⁵_____ 300, please.
A OK. The total price is £250.
B Does that ⁶_____ delivery?
A Yes, it does.
B Great. Can you ⁷_____ my order by email?
A Sure. I'll ⁸_____ you now.

# Practically speaking

**Complete the sentences with the numbers. Then say the numbers.**

27     53,000*     11     60,000,000*

1  The population of Italy is _____ .
2  The number of employees at Google is

_____ .

3  The number of countries in the European Union is

_____ .

4  The number of people in a football team is

_____ .

*Numbers are approximate.

## Language at work | Present simple: *he / she / it*

### Present simple: *he / she / it*

**Form**

**Positive:**

| He | makes | products. |
|----|-------|-----------|
| She | designs | clothes. |
| It | sells | cars. |

**Negative:**

| He | doesn't make | products. |
|----|-------|-----------|
| She | doesn't design | clothes. |
| It | doesn't sell | cars. |

**Questions:**

| Does | he make products? |
|------|-------------------|
| Does | she design clothes? |
| Does | it sell cars? |

**Short answers:**

Yes, he / she / it does.
No, he / she / it doesn't.

> He **designs** cars.
>
> She **doesn't sell** clothes.
>
> A **Does** he **make** products?     B  Yes, he **does**.
>
> A **Does** the company **sell** cars?   B  No, it **doesn't**.

**Careful!**

He doesn't make cars. ✓     ~~He doesn't makes cars.~~ ✗

### Spelling

Most verbs: verb + -*s*

> He *makes / sells / builds / designs*.

Verbs ending in -*o*: *It does.*

Exception: *have* → *has*

> We have an online store. → The company **has** an online store.

---

**1  Complete the sentences with the correct form of the verbs in (brackets).**

1  He _____ (export) cars to other countries.
2  She _____ (sell) electronics in the store.
3  It _____ (build) houses.
4  He _____ (not / import) cars from other countries.
5  She _____ (not / buy) electronics.
6  It _____ (not / build) aeroplanes.
7  The company _____ (have) three factories.

**2  Underline the correct verb in *italics*.**

1  Gazprom *sell / sells* oil and gas.
2  I *sell / sells* cars.
3  It *design / designs* houses.
4  We *deliver / delivers* products.
5  The company *don't have / doesn't have* an online store.
6  They *don't make / doesn't make* mobiles.

**3  Make questions with the verbs in (brackets). Complete the short answers.**

1  A _____ Toyota _____ cars? (make)
   B  Yes, it _____ .
2  A _____ Apple _____ food? (deliver)
   B  No, it _____ .
3  A _____ Walmart _____ food and clothes? (sell)
   B  Yes, it _____ .

**4  Complete the questions with *do* or *does*.**

1  _____ you have the item number?
2  What products _____ the company export to China?
3  Where _____ she buy the clothes?
4  _____ Simon and Sue work in this department?
5  Who _____ you work for?
6  _____ the price include delivery?

# Working with words

**1 Look at the pictures and complete the word puzzle.**

1 | c | | | | e | |
2 | | | a | | | | | | i | |
3 | | n | | | | | a | | |
4 | | o | | | | | | | a | |
5 | | e | | | | | | d | | |
6 | | | |
7 | | | a | |
8 | | | | n | | | u | | |

**2 Complete with the phrases.**

> I'd like (x2)   can I have    that's (x2)
> would you like   can I help you

A  Hello, ¹_____?

B  What ²_____, Ana?

C  ³_____ vegetable lasagne and salad, please. And mineral water.

B  And ⁴_____ a cheese sandwich and chocolate cake? And ⁵_____ tea.

A  So, ⁶_____ vegetable lasagne and salad, a cheese sandwich, chocolate cake, mineral water, and tea. ⁷_____ 19 dollars, please.

**3 Put the words in the right order.**

1  food / like / do / What / you
_____?

2  steak / like / I / fries / and
_____.

3  don't / Mexican / I / like / food
_____.

4  but / like / rice / don't / I / pasta / like / I
_____.

5  Japanese / Do / like / food / you
_____?

6  like / Chinese / I / food
_____.

# Business communication

**1 Put the conversations in the right order.**

1  a  ___  At seven thirty?

   b  ___  There's a new Indian restaurant in town. Would you like to have dinner?

   c  _1_  Do you like Indian food?

   d  ___  OK. Sure. See you in reception at seven thirty.

   e  ___  Yes, please. That would be nice. What time?

   f  ___  Yes, I love it.

2  a  ___  What time can you play?

   b  ___  Sure. See you at three thirty.

   c  ___  I'd love to, but I'm afraid I'm busy at two.

   d  ___  Is three thirty OK?

   e  _1_  Do you want to play tennis today at two?

**2 Put the words in the right order to make questions.**

1  you / Would / dinner / Tuesday / have / like / to / on?
_____?

2  meet / time / What / you / can?
_____?

3  play / you / want / to / Do / tennis / Wednesday / on?
_____?

4  two / OK / thirty / Is?
_____?

5  you / day / can / play / What?
_____?

**3 Match the questions in 2 to the answers.**

a  ___  I'm afraid I'm busy at two thirty.

b  ___  I can play on Friday.

c  ___  That'd be great. Thanks. What time on Tuesday?

d  ___  At eleven thirty.

e  ___  I'd love to, but I can't on Wednesday.

## Practically speaking

**1 Put the days of the week in the right order.**

| Saturday | Tuesday | Thursday |
|----------|---------|----------|
| Sunday | Wednesday | Friday |

Monday _____ _____ _____ _____

_____ _____

**2 Match 1–5 to a–e.**

| | | | |
|---|---|---|---|
| 1 | 8.00 ____ | a | I have lunch at twelve thirty. |
| 2 | 10.45 ____ | b | I finish work at five thirty. |
| 3 | 7.00 ____ | c | I have coffee at ten forty-five. |
| 4 | 12.30 ____ | d | I start work at eight. |
| 5 | 5.30 ____ | e | I have dinner at seven. |

## Language at work | can / can't

### can / can't

**Form**

**Positive:**

| | | |
|---|---|---|
| I | | |
| You | | speak English. |
| He / She | can | play tennis. |
| We | | sing. |
| They | | |

**Negative:**

| | | |
|---|---|---|
| I | | |
| You | | play golf. |
| He / She | can't | run a marathon. |
| We | | cook. |
| They | | |

**Questions:**

Can you play the guitar?
Can she speak Japanese?
Can they play a musical instrument?

**Short answers:**

Yes, I / you / he / she / it / we / they can.
No, I / you / he / she / it / we / they can't.

**Questions with question words:**

| | | |
|---|---|---|
| What sports | | he play? |
| What languages | can | you speak? |
| What type of food | | they cook? |

A *Can you play* tennis?    B *Yes, I can. / No, I can't.*
We *can't cook* Japanese food.
A *What languages can he speak?*
B *He can speak Polish and English.*

**1 Write sentences with *can* (+) or *can't* (–).**

1 play the guitar (+)
   *I can play the guitar* .

2 cook (–)
   She _____ .

3 run a marathon (–)
   They _____ .

4 play a musical instrument (+)
   I _____ .

5 play tennis (+)
   He _____ .

**2 Write questions with *can*. Complete the short answers.**

1 you / English / speak
   *Can you speak English?*
   Yes, *I can* .

2 cook / he / food / Indian
   _____ ?
   No, _____ .

3 the / she / guitar / play
   _____ ?
   No, _____ .

4 other / speak / she / languages
   _____ ?
   Yes, _____ .

**3 Underline the correct word(s) in *italics*.**

1 I *don't can / can't* play golf.
2 *Does he can / Can he* play a musical instrument?
3 She *can't / doesn't can* cook Indian food.
4 *Do you can / Can you* speak English?
5 Karl can play the guitar, but he *can't / doesn't can* sing.

**4 Put the words in the right order to make questions.**

1 play / can / sports / you / What
   _____ ?

2 speak / she / What / can / languages
   _____ ?

3 type / What / Simon / of / can / food / cook
   _____ ?

4 instrument / play / they / musical / What / can
   _____ ?

**5 Match the questions from 4 to the answers.**

a ____ Simon can cook Italian food, but he can't cook Mexican food.

b ____ They can play the guitar and the piano.

c ____ Claudine can speak three languages: French, German, and English.

d ____ I can play football and tennis, but I can't play golf.

## Working with words

**1 Look at the technology. Complete the words.**

1 l \_\_ \_\_ \_\_ \_\_ p
2 w \_\_ \_\_ \_\_ \_\_ m
3 h \_\_ \_\_ \_\_ \_\_ \_\_ t
4 p \_\_ \_\_ \_\_ \_\_ \_\_ \_\_ \_\_ r
5 p \_\_ \_\_ \_\_ \_\_ \_\_ r

**2 Complete with the words.**

USB stick    smartphone    computer    digital camera

1 I can photograph machines with a _____ .
2 Please call this number on your _____ .
3 When I travel, I have my documents on a
_____ .
4 I use an old _____ , but I want a
modern tablet!

**3 Underline the correct verb in *italics*.**

---

**Subject:** Your presentation

---

Dear Arnie

Here is the link to the presentation. [1] *Switch on / Click*
the link and then [2] *enter / scan* your password.
[3] *Connect / Download* the PowerPoint presentation
from the website. You can [4] *print / save* the
presentation on a USB stick or [5] *click / connect* your
laptop to the projector.

Also find attached the documents for your presentation.
[6] *Print / Enter* the documents for the clients.

Good luck with the presentation!

Sally

## Business communication

**1 Complete with the question words.**

How    What    Where    Do    Is    Does

a _____'s the problem?
b _____ does it work?
c _____ you have a laptop?
d _____ the projector on?
e _____ it work now?
f _____ do I switch it on?

**2 Complete the conversation with questions a–f from 1.**

A  Can you help me?
B  Sure. [1]_____?
A  I don't know how to use this projector.
[2]_____?
B  [3]_____?
A  No, it isn't.
B  First, you need to switch it on.
A  Yes, but [4]_____?
B  Here. [5]_____?
A  Yes, it does.
B  Great. [6]_____?
A  No, I don't. My presentation is on this USB stick.

**3 Complete the instructions.**

[1]F_____ , scan the designs. [2]T_____ , save
the document on your laptop. [3]N_____ , attach the
document to an email. You [4]n_____ to send the
email to me and to Peter in Rome.

**4 Tick (✓) the correct response, a or b.**

1 What's the problem with the projector?
  a  I don't use it.
  b  I don't know how to use it.
2 How does it work?
  a  I don't know.
  b  No, I don't.
3 Where do I switch it on?
  a  Press.
  b  Here.
4 Is the Internet on?
  a  I think so.
  b  I think yes.
5 How do I start the software?
  a  You need click *enter*.
  b  You need to click *enter*.

# Practically speaking

**Look at the pictures. Complete the sentences with *this*, *that*, *these*, or *those*.**

1

_____'s your office.

2

_____ are my documents.

3

_____ are your colleague's desks.

4

_____ is my phone.

## Language at work | Possessive adjectives

### Possessive adjectives

**Form**

| | |
|---|---|
| I | my |
| you | your |
| he | his |
| she | her |
| it | its |
| we | our |
| they | their |

*It's **my** car.*

***Your** company is in Spain.*

*Is this **his** pen?*

*It isn't **her** desk.*

***Our** factory is modern.*

*Are **their** offices here?*

### Possessive 's

For names of people, add possessive *'s*.

the office of Nigel = *Nigel's office*

the office of Atif and Giulio = *Atif and Giulio's office*.

**Careful!**

| Possessive *'s*: | *Ben's car* = the car of Ben |
|---|---|
| Verb *be*: | *Ben's in the car.* = Ben is in the car. |

---

**1 Complete with the possessive adjectives.**

our    his    your    her    my    their    its

1  I'm from Germany, but _____ job is in France.
2  You have a meeting at ten and _____ interview is at twelve.
3  We have a sales office in London, but _____ head office is in Dubai.
4  He is in reception, but _____ interview is after lunch.
5  She works at home and _____ boss works in an office.
6  They sell electronics and _____ customers buy the products from the online store.
7  The USB stick is small but _____ memory is big.

**2 Underline the correct word in *italics*.**

1  What's *you / your* name?
2  *I / My* job is good.
3  *I / My* name's Piotr.
4  *It's / Its* a bad projector.
5  *She / Her* smartphone doesn't work.
6  *His / He's* out of the office at the moment.
7  *We / Our* video conference is at three.
8  *They / Their* use our printer.

**3 Write the possessive *'s* in the sentences.**

1  Is this Mike headset?
2  Juliette and Medhat office is here.
3  Rosa computer is on, so she's here.
4  Where is Remi, Sultan, and Ricardo meeting today?

**4 Correct the mistakes.**

1  He's name is Mike.

_____

2  Is this I new mobile?

_____

3  Hello. This is Nigel voicemail.

_____

4  The printer is old and its slow.

_____

5  Their office is there and are office is here.

_____

## Working with words

**1** Match the pictures to the words. Write the letter.

1 bus ___
2 car ___
3 train ___
4 taxi ___
5 plane ___
6 bicycle ___
7 motorcycle ___

**2** Complete the travel words.

1 t __ r m __ n __ l
2 r __ c __ __ p t
3 __ - t __ c k __ t
4 b __ g
5 p __ s s p __ r t
6 b __ __ r d __ n g g __ t __
7 f l __ g h t

**3** <u>Underline</u> the correct verb in *italics*.

1 Can I *have / check in* your passport and e-ticket, please?
2 Please *arrive / go* to the boarding gate at nine fifteen.
3 That's ten pounds. Do you *have / want* a receipt?
4 Can you *take / go* me to the airport?
5 What time does the flight *arrive / go* in Berlin?
6 Which terminal do you *check in / want*?
7 Your flight *takes / leaves* at two forty-five.
8 Do you have any bags to *check in / go*?

## Business communication

**1** Complete the emails with the phrases.

I can't meet    I'd like to arrange    is fine for me
Can we meet on    we arrange a new date and time

**To:** Regina; Laurent

1 _____ a
meeting about the new project in March.
2 _____
Wednesday 21st September at 9.30 a.m.?

Best regards

Federico

---

Dear Federico

I'm sorry, 3 _____ on
Wednesday 21st September. I'm at a sales conference.
Can 4 _____?

Kind regards

Regina

---

Hi Federico

Wednesday 21st 5 _____ .
See you at 9.30 a.m.

Regards

Laurent

**2** Put the words in the right order.

1 a meeting / I'd / arrange / like / to

_____ .

2 sorry / can't / I / at 2 p.m. / meet / I'm

_____ .

3 you / on Monday / Are / free / at 3.30 p.m.

_____ ?

4 fine / 13th April / me / is / for

_____ .

**3** Put the conversation in the right order.

a ___ Sorry, I'm busy on Monday. I'm visiting a new client.
b ___ Yes, sure. See you on Tuesday 27th at one thirty.
c _1_ Hi, Regina. Are you free on Monday 26th September?
d ___ Is one thirty OK for you?
e ___ How about Tuesday afternoon?
f ___ Yes, I'm free on Tuesday. What time is good for you?

## Practically speaking

**Match the dates to the sentences.**

1  3rd September ____
2  7/3 ____
3  2nd February ____
4  31/5 ____
5  24th December ____

a  My birthday is on the thirty-first of May.
b  Our trip to Munich is on the second of February.
c  I'm on holiday on the twenty-fourth of December.
d  We have a project meeting on the seventh of March.
e  The factory visit is on the third of September.

## Language at work | *was / were*

### *was / were*

**Form**

**Positive:**

| I | | |
|---|---|---|
| He / She | was | in Oman last Thursday. |
| It | | |
| You | | |
| We | were | in Barcelona for four days. |
| They | | |

**Negative:**

| I | | |
|---|---|---|
| He / She | wasn't | in Rio yesterday. |
| It | | |
| You | | |
| We | weren't | there last week. |
| They | | |

**Questions:**

Was he / she / it in Lima last weekend?
Were you / we / they there last Tuesday?

**Short answers:**

| Yes, he / she / it was. | No, he / she / it wasn't. |
|---|---|
| Yes, you / we / they were. | No, you / we / they weren't. |

**Questions with question words:**

Where were you yesterday?
When were you in Rome?
How was your trip?

> I **was** in Tokyo on Monday.
>
> We **weren't** in London last week.
>
> *A* **Was** she on holiday yesterday?    *B* Yes, she **was**.
>
> *A* Where **were** they last Friday?    *B* They **were** at a conference.

---

**1  Complete with *was / were* (+) or *wasn't / weren't* (−).**

1  I _____ in Peru last week. +
2  She _____ in Dubai yesterday. −
3  They _____ there for three days. +
4  The meeting _____ very useful. −
5  We _____ there very long. −
6  He _____ on holiday last weekend. +

**2  Write questions with *was / were*. Complete the short answers.**

1  you / in Barcelona / last week
   *Were you in Barcelona last week?*
   Yes, _I was_ .
2  they / busy / yesterday
   _____?
   No, _____ .
3  he / there / last week
   _____?
   No, _____ .
4  the city / quiet / last night
   _____?
   Yes, _____ .

**3  Underline the correct verb in *italics*.**

A  [1] *Were / Was* you here last week?
B  No, I [2] *weren't / wasn't*. I [3] *were / was* in Japan for six days.
A  How [4] *was / were* your trip?
B  The sales conference [5] *were / was* very useful, but the meetings with clients [6] *wasn't / weren't*. And you? [7] *Was / Were* you busy?
A  No, I [8] *weren't / wasn't*. I [9] *was / were* on holiday for four days!

**4  Put the words in the right order to make questions.**

1  Monday / you / last / were / Where
   _____?
2  in / they / When / Santiago / were?
   _____?
3  How long / was / Dubai / in / she
   _____?
4  your / How / trip / business / was
   _____?

**5  Match the questions in 4 to the answers.**

a  ____ OK. The meetings with clients were very useful.
b  ____ In Barcelona. I was there for three days.
c  ____ She was in Dubai for two days.
d  ____ They were in Santiago last Tuesday and Wednesday.

Practice file 8 | Travel

## File 01 | Unit 4

**Business communication, Exercise 5, page 26**

**Student A**

1 You work in Production. Call Karla Herzog in Human Resources. You want two new employees in your department. You want Karla to call back as soon as possible. Your mobile number is 0556 476 38744.
2 You work in Sales. Henrik Mortensen is your manager, but he is out. Answer the telephone and take a message.

## File 02 | Unit 8

**Business communication, Exercise 6, page 50**

**Student A**

Look at your notes.

| What? | Sales meeting |
|---|---|
| When? | Monday 25th January |
| Time? | 11.30 a.m. |

Call Student B. Arrange a meeting.

***Example:*** *Hello, I'd like to arrange a sales meeting on …*

## File 03 | Unit 5

**Language at work, Exercise 11, page 31**

**Student A**

1 Ask questions about Zara. Complete the table.
   ***Examples:*** **A** *Does the company make products?*
   **B** *Yes, it does.*
   **A** *What products does it make?*
   **B** *It makes clothes.*

| Company | Zara |
|---|---|
| Company products | |
| Company activity | |
| Factories | |
| Stores | |

2 Answer questions about Fiat.

**Company:** Fiat
**Company products:** cars and car engines
**Company activity:** designs / makes / exports cars
**Factories:** Italy, Brazil, Argentina, and Poland
**Stores:** an online store

## File 04 | Unit 7

**Business communication, Exercise 5, page 44**

**Student A**

**Student B doesn't know how to scan documents on a new printer. Look at the pictures and words. Give instructions.**

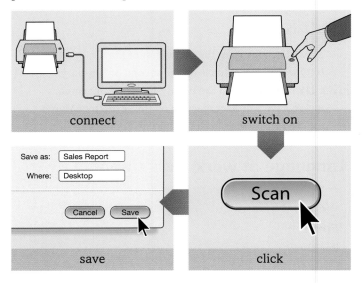

connect | switch on

Save as: Sales Report
Where: Desktop
Cancel | Save

Scan

save | click

## File 05 | Unit 8

**Language at work, Exercise 8, page 49**

**Student A**

1 This is Student B's diary for last week. Ask questions with these words and complete the diary.

   Where … last Monday?

   When … in Hong Kong?

   Where … last Thursday?

   How long … in …?

   Monday – In _____
   _____ and _____ – In Hong Kong
   Thursday, _____, and _____
   – In _____

2 This is your diary for last week. Answer Student B's questions.

   Saturday – In Rio
   Sunday and Monday – In Lima
   Tuesday, Wednesday, and Thursday
   – In Santiago

# File 06 | Unit 4

**Business communication, Exercise 5, page 26**

**Student B**

1 You work in Human Resources. Karla Herzog is your manager, but she is out. Answer the telephone and take a message.
2 You work in Finance. Call Henrik Mortensen in Sales. You want sales information for this month. You want Henrik to call back as soon as possible. Your mobile number is 0657 671 1156.

# File 07 | Unit 2

**Working with words, Exercise 11, page 11**

**Student A**

1 You are Elias. Answer Student B's questions.

> **Name:** Elias Bauer
> **Country:** Germany
> **Company:** Alterlink
> **Head office:** Vienna, Austria

2 Student B is Rita Epstein. Ask questions. Complete the card.

> **Name:** Rita Epstein
> **Country:** _____
> **Company:** _____
> **Head office:** _____

# File 08 | Unit 7

**Language at work, Exercise 7, page 43**

**Student B**

1 Ask Student A about these objects. Match to the names and places.
   *smartphone    USB stick    projector    laptop*

   Juliette / desk _____
   Andrey / office _____
   the manager / desk _____
   Medhat and Sultan / office _____

   ***Example:*** *A Is my smartphone on Juliette's desk?*
   *B No, it isn't on her desk.*
   *A Is it in Medhat and Sultan's office?*
   *B Yes, it is in their office.*

2 Choose an object for each name and place.
   *webcam    digital camera    printer    tablet*

   Juliette's desk _____
   Andrey's office _____
   the manager's desk _____
   Medhat and Sultan's office _____

3 Answer Student A's questions about each object.

# File 09 | Unit 5

**Language at work, Exercise 11, page 31**

**Student B**

1 Answer questions about Zara.

> **Company:** Zara
> **Company products:** clothes
> **Company activity:** makes/sells clothes
> **Factories:** Spain and Portugal
> **Stores:** 450

2 Ask questions about Fiat. Complete the table
   ***Examples:*** *A Does the company make products?*
   *B Yes, it does.*
   *A What products does it make?*
   *B It makes cars.*

| Company | Fiat |
|---|---|
| Company products | |
| Company activity | |
| Factories | |
| Stores | |

# File 10 | Unit 7

**Business communication, Exercise 5, page 44**

**Student B**

**Student A doesn't know how to download photographs from a digital camera to a laptop.**

**Look at the pictures and words. Give instructions.**

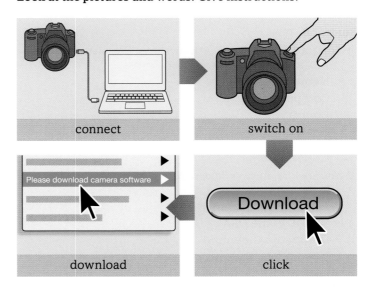

connect

switch on

Please download camera software

download

Download

click

## File 11 | Unit 8

**Language at work, Exercise 8, page 49**

**Student B**

1 This is your diary for last week. Answer Student A's questions.

> Monday – In Tokyo
> Tuesday and Wednesday –
>  In Hong Kong
> Thursday, Friday, and Saturday –
>  In Beijing

2 This is Student A's diary for last week. Ask questions with these words and complete the diary.

Where … last Saturday?
When … in Lima?
Where … last Tuesday?
How long … in …?

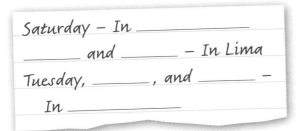

> Saturday – In _____
> _____ and _____ – In Lima
> Tuesday, _____, and _____ –
>  In _____

## File 12 | Unit 2

**Working with words, Exercise 11, page 11**

**Student B**

1 Student A is Elias Bauer. Ask questions. Complete the card.

> **Name:** Elias Bauer
> **Company:** _____
> **Country:** _____
> **Head office:** _____

2 You are Rita. Answer Student A's questions.

> **Name:** Rita Epstein
> **Country:** the USA
> **Company:** Greenbird
> **Head office:** Toronto, Canada

## File 13 | Unit 8

**Activity, page 51**

**Pair B**

1 Read information 1–3. Complete your calendar below.

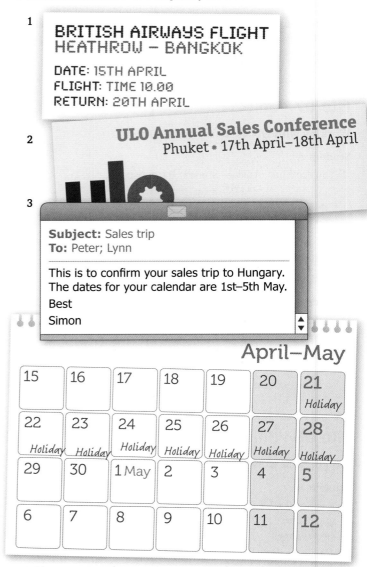

1
**BRITISH AIRWAYS FLIGHT
HEATHROW – BANGKOK**
DATE: 15TH APRIL
FLIGHT: TIME 10.00
RETURN: 20TH APRIL

2
**ULO Annual Sales Conference**
Phuket * 17th April–18th April

3
**Subject:** Sales trip
**To:** Peter; Lynn

This is to confirm your sales trip to Hungary. The dates for your calendar are 1st–5th May.
Best
Simon

April–May

| 15 | 16 | 17 | 18 | 19 | 20 | 21 Holiday |
| 22 Holiday | 23 Holiday | 24 Holiday | 25 Holiday | 26 Holiday | 27 Holiday | 28 Holiday |
| 29 | 30 | 1 May | 2 | 3 | 4 | 5 |
| 6 | 7 | 8 | 9 | 10 | 11 | 12 |

2 70▷ Listen to a voicemail message. Write the information in your calendar.

3 Have a teleconference with Pair A. Arrange a date for a meeting.

## File 14 | Unit 8

**Business communication, Exercise 6, page 50**

**Student B**

Student A calls you to arrange a meeting. You are busy on Monday 25th January. You are visiting a factory. Ask for a different date and time.

# File 15 | Unit 3

**Activity, page 21**

**Student B / Team B**

| | | | |
|---|---|---|---|
| No, they're in the car park. | Is the factory new or old? | Yes, it is. | Where is the head office? |
| Is Claudia in the warehouse? | They're in Dubai. | Is your office big? | He's in the cafeteria. |

# File 16 | Unit 2

**Language at work, Exercise 6, page 13**

**Student B**

1 Look at the map. Answer Student A about Ricardo, Lokas, and Chen.

*Example:*  **A** *Is Ricardo in the Portugal office?*
   **B** *No, he isn't.*
   **A** *Is he in the Brazil office?*
   **B** *Yes, he is.*

2 Ask Student A about Rachel, Maya, and Alex.

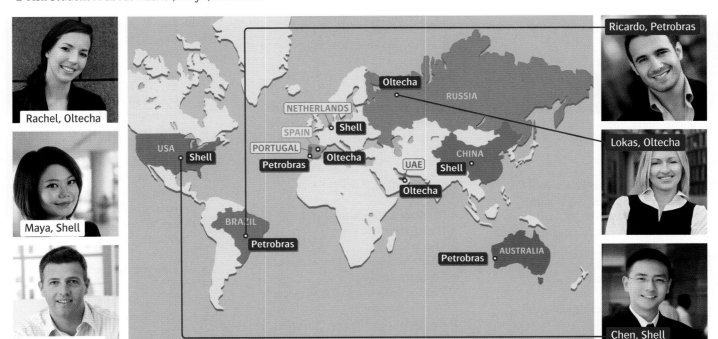

# Unit 1

## 01

**Luis** Hello, I'm Luis Moreira.
**Fabienne** Hello, my name's Fabienne Mercier.

**Tageshi** Hello, I'm Tageshi.
**Paula** Hi, I'm Paula.

## 02

1 IT technician
2 finance director
3 office assistant
4 sales representative
5 engineer
6 human resources manager

## 03

technician
director
assistant
representative
manager
engineer

## 04

**Fabienne** I'm a human resources manager. What's your job, Luis?
**Luis** Oh, I'm a finance director.

**Paula** What's your job, Tageshi?
**Tageshi** I'm an IT technician. And you?
**Paula** I'm an office assistant.

## 05

**Jacob** Hi, I'm Jacob.
**Kenji** I'm Kenji. Hello.
**Jacob** And you're Alice.
**Maria** No, I'm not Alice. I'm Maria.
**Jacob** Sorry. You're Alice.
**Alice** Yes. Hello.

## 06

**Jacob** Are you an office assistant?
**Maria** Yes, I am. Are you a human resources manager?
**Jacob** No, I'm not. I'm a finance director.

## 07

**A** Hello. Are you Tomas?
**B** No, I'm not.
**A** Are you an IT technician?
**B** No, I'm not.
**A** What's your name?
**B** My name's Enzo.
**A** Are you a sales representative?
**B** No, I'm not.
**A** Are you a sales manager?
**B** Yes, I am.
**A** So, you're Enzo Silva.
**B** Yes.

## 08

A B C D E F G H I J K L M
N O P Q R S T U V W X Y Z

## 09

**Assistant** David?
**Manager** Yes?
**Assistant** Is Steven's surname Azikiwe or Azakawe?
**Manager** Azikiwe.
**Assistant** Can you spell that?
**Manager** It's A-Z-I-K-I-W-E.
**Assistant** A-Z-I-K-I-W-E. Azikiwe. Thanks. Oh. And one more. Mrs Borysiak. What's the first name?
**Manager** Er … Gabryjela.
**Assistant** Oh! Can you spell that?
**Manager** G-A-B-R-Y-J-E-L-A.
**Assistant** G-A-B-R-Y-J-E-L-A. Thanks.

## 10

1 **Franco** Good morning. Are you Kasia?
  **Kasia** Yes, I am.
  **Franco** I'm Franco. Nice to meet you.
  **Kasia** Nice to meet you too.
2 **Sally** Hello, Franco.
  **Franco** Hi, Sally. Kasia, this is Sally, my assistant.
  **Kasia** Good afternoon, Sally. Nice to meet you.
  **Sally** Nice to meet you too, Kasia.
3 **Franco** See you soon, Kasia.
  **Kasia** Yes, see you soon. And it was nice meeting you, Sally. Goodbye.
  **Sally/Franco** Bye.

## 11

1 Good morning. Are you Kasia?
  Yes, I am.
2 I'm Franco. Nice to meet you.
  Nice to meet you too.
3 This is Sally.
  Good afternoon, Sally. Nice to meet you.
4 See you soon.
  Yes, see you soon. And it was nice meeting you, Sally.
5 Goodbye.
  Bye.

# Unit 2

## 12

**Saleh** Hello. Are you Ricardo Ferreira?
**Ricardo** Yes, I am.
**Saleh** My name's Saleh Al-Banwan. I work for Zain.
**Ricardo** Oh, nice to meet you.
**Saleh** I'm an engineer in the head office in Kuwait. Here's my card.

## 13

1 **A** Hello, I'm Alex. I work for Santander.
  **B** Nice to meet you.
2 **A** Hi, I'm Jae Min. I'm a marketing assistant.
  **B** What's your company?
  **A** It's Asiana Airlines.
3 **A** What's your name?
  **B** Ricardo Ferreira.
  **A** Nice to meet you, Ricardo. I'm Jae Min.
  **B** Nice to meet you too. My company is Petrobras. Here's my card.
  **A** Thanks.

## 14

Spain
China
Brazil
Japan
Kuwait
Germany
South Korea
the USA
Saudi Arabia

## 15

1 **A** Where are you from, Saleh?
  **B** I'm from Saudi Arabia.
  **A** Where's your head office?
  **B** It's in Kuwait.
2 **A** My name's Alex. I'm from the USA.
  **B** What's your company?
  **A** My company is Santander. It's a bank in Spain.
3 **A** Hi, Jae Min. Are you from South Korea?
  **B** Yes, I am.
  **A** Where's your head office?
  **B** It's in Seoul.
4 **A** Where are you from, Ricardo?
  **B** I'm from Brazil and I work for Petrobras.
  **A** Where's your head office?
  **B** It's in Rio de Janeiro.

## 16

**A** Hello, I work for Oltecha.
**B** Nice to meet you. My company is Petrobras.
**A** Is your head office in São Paulo?
**B** No, it isn't. It's in Rio. Where's your company?
**A** I work in São Paulo and the company head office is in Stavanger.
**B** Is Stavanger in Norway?
**A** Yes, it is.

## 17

0 1 2 3 4 5 6 7 8 9

## 18

0 7 8 5 4 2

## 19

6 7 2 0

## 20

1 Flight BA 3710 for Paris is boarding. That's British Airways flight 3710.
2 The security code for my company is 2828. That's 2828.
3 My credit card number is 4162 7409 3708 2358. Let me repeat that. 4162 7409 3708 2358.
4 My passport number is 654218792. That's 654218792.

## 21

**A** Good morning. Inditex Spain.
**B** Good morning. Can I speak to Aitur Garitano, please?
**A** Yes, of course. One moment.
**B** Thanks.

## 22

1 **Maria** Hello?
**Caller** Hi. Is that Rosa?
**Maria** No, it isn't. It's Maria.
**Caller** Oh, is Rosa there?
**Maria** No, I'm sorry, she's out.
**Caller** OK. Thanks.
2 **Maria** Good afternoon, Maria speaking.
**Caller** Hello. Is Rosa in the office?
**Maria** Yes, sure. One moment.
**Caller** Thanks.

# Unit 3

## 23

Mieszanka is a company in Poland. The sales office is in Warsaw. The head office is in Katowice. The old factory is also here. The new factory is in Poznań. It's a factory with a big warehouse, new offices, a car park, and a good cafeteria.

## 24

a warehouse
a factory
a cafeteria
a reception
an office
a car park

## 25

1 **A** Is your sales office in London?
**B** Yes, it is. It's small, but it's in the centre of London.
2 **A** Where's your company?
**B** The head office is in Milan, but the factory and the warehouse are in Turin. They are old, but they are big.
3 **A** Where's the cafeteria?
**B** Here.
**A** Is it good?
**B** Yes. It's small, but the food is good.

## 26

1 **A** Hello.
**B** Hello. We're here for Mike Thompson. My name's Sonia Jones and this is Bill Dare.
**A** OK. What's your company?
**B** Introcom.
**A** OK. One moment.
2 **C** Hello. Mike Thompson.
**A** Hello, Mike. It's Gill. Two people are here for you.
**C** Who are they?
**A** Sonia Jones and Bill Dare from Introcom.
**C** Oh yes, of course. Thanks, Gill.
3 **C** Hello, Sonia.
**B** Hello, Mike. Nice to see you again.
**C** Where's Bill?
**B** He's in the cafeteria.
**C** Oh, OK. Let's have a coffee then.

## 27

1 www dot bp dot com
2 www dot jbs dot com dot br
3 www dot toyota dash global dot com
4 d dot roberts at fisons dot co dot uk
5 juan underscore mata at nike dot com

## 28

**A** My address is d dot roberts at fisons dot co dot uk.
**B** Can you repeat that?
**A** Yes, it's d dot roberts at fisons dot co dot uk.
**B** Thanks.

## 29

Can you repeat that?

# Unit 4

## 30

**Joanna** My name's Joanna. I'm from Hungary and I live in Sopron. I work for a software company. We make CD-ROMs and DVDs. I'm a sales rep and I meet customers. I sell the products to training companies and schools. We have three people in the Sales Department. I work in West Hungary and Austria.
**Fred** My name's Fred Meesmaecker. I'm from France, but I live in England. I work for Capgemini. It's a global company. We have over 300 offices in more than 40 countries. I'm a project manager and I manage a team of IT technicians. I have eight people in my team and they manage computer systems for the client. This month, we have a project with a food company.

## 31

work
live
make
manage
meet
have
sell

## 32

Logistics
Sales
Production
IT
Finance
Human Resources

## 33

departments
customers
products
companies
offices
technicians
employees
people
countries

## 34

**Karla** Good afternoon. Thank you for coming. Let's start with introductions. My name's Karla and I manage the Human Resources Department. And you're Astrid?

**Astrid** Yes.

**Karla** Where are you from, Astrid?

**Astrid** I'm from Switzerland, but I don't live there.

**Karla** Where do you live?

**Astrid** I live in Germany with my husband. We live in Munich.

**Karla** Right. Do you work in Sales?

**Astrid** Yes, I do.

**Karla** Great, thanks, Astrid. … And what do you do?

**Mark** Hi. My name's Mark. I work in Finance.

**Karla** Thanks, Mark. Do you live in the USA?

**Mark** No, I don't. I live in Canada. I'm from Vancouver.

## 35

**Martha** Sales. Hello?

**Janusz** Hi. Is Liko there?

**Martha** No, I'm sorry, he's out. Can I take a message?

**Janusz** Yes, it's Janusz in IT.

**Martha** Oh, hi. This is Martha. I'm the new sales assistant.

**Janusz** Hi, Martha. I'm calling about the new sales website.

**Martha** Sorry, one moment. OK. Go ahead. What's the message for Liko?

**Janusz** It's about the sales website. Do you want dot com or dot co dot uk in the address?

**Martha** Sorry. I don't understand. Can you repeat that?

**Janusz** The new website is www dot synox dash sales, but do you want synox dash sales dot com or synox dash sales dot co dot uk?

**Martha** OK. Is there anything else?

**Janusz** Yes. Please call me back as soon as possible. My mobile number is 07700 897 833.

**Martha** So that's 07700 897 833.

**Janusz** That's right.

**Martha** OK. I'll give Liko your message.

**Janusz** Thanks, Martha.

## 36

1 Hello. My name's Raul Avasthi. That's A-V-A-S-T-H-I. I work for Tinto Insurance. We have a software problem in the office in Dubai. Can you call 00941 775 7568? Thanks.

2 Hi. This is Emily in HR. Sorry, I have a problem with my car, so I'm late. Can you tell my team?

3 It's Jan Wilders in Rotterdam. Sorry, but there's a problem with your new software. I'm not in my office so call my mobile. It's 0031 476 4857. That's 0031 476 4857. It's very urgent!

# Unit 5

## 37

1 I work for Gazprom. It's an energy company. We sell oil and gas.

2 I work for Dassault. It's an aeronautical company. We make and sell aeroplanes.

3 I work for Aldi. It's a retail company. We sell food.

4 I work for Toyota. It's an automobile company. We make and sell cars.

5 I work for Samsung. It's an electronics company. We make and sell televisions and mobiles.

## 38

Embraer is a Brazilian company. We make and sell aeroplanes. We have factories in Brazil and sales offices all over the world. In the factories we build aeroplanes. We also design new products by computer in the R&D Department. We export products to China, the USA, and Europe.

Uniqlo is a Japanese company. We sell clothes. We have stores in 13 countries around the world. Customers visit the stores and buy the products. We also have an online store. Customers order products online. Then we deliver the products to the customer.

## 39

1 buy
2 export
3 design
4 deliver
5 build
6 order

## 40

Auchan is a retail company. It sells food and clothes. It has stores in Europe and Asia. The head office is in Croix, France. Martin Reuland works for Auchan, but he doesn't work in the head office. He is a store manager in Calais.

LG is an electronics company. It makes and sells televisions and mobile phones. Soo Jin Lee works in the R&D Department in Seoul. She designs new products. LG has over 20 factories in eleven countries and exports products all over the world.

## 41

1 Does Martin work in Croix?
No, he doesn't.

2 Does LG export products?
Yes, it does.

3 Does Auchan have stores in Africa?
No, it doesn't.

4 Does Soo Jin Lee design new products?
Yes, she does.

5 Does she work in the Sales Department?
No, she doesn't.

## 42

10 11 12 13 14 15 16 17 18 19
20 30 40 50 60 70 80 90 100 1,000

## 43

27 82 145 610 3,900 21,340 172,000
58,000,000

## 44

1 There are 1,600 employees in my company.
2 We export 250 cars a week.
3 Brazil has a population of 424,000,000.
4 We have 59 factories in 14 countries.

## 45

A Hello, Euroboxes. Paul Rice speaking. Can I help you?
B Hi, it's Carel Peeters from Equest. I'd like to order Standard Single Wall boxes.
A One moment, please. Do you have the item number?
B Yes, it's SSW dash 3411.
A Thanks. One box is 20 cents. How many would you like?
B 10,000.
A So that's … 2,000 euros.
B Does that include delivery?
A Yes, it does.
B OK. And I also want 5,000 medium. The item number is SSW dash 3412. What's the price?
A One box is 25 cents. … That's 1,250 euros.
B OK. That's fine.
A Right, so that's 10,000 small. And 5,000 medium. The total price is 3,250 euros.
B Can you confirm my order by email?
A Yes, of course. What's your email, Carel?
B It's C dot peeters. P-E-E-T-E-R-S at Equest dot co dot be.
A I'll email that now.
B Thanks very much.

## Unit 6

## 46

1 steak and fries
2 mineral water
3 tea
4 chicken curry and rice
5 ice cream
6 cheese sandwich
7 orange juice
8 coffee
9 tomato soup with bread
10 salad
11 vegetable lasagne
12 chocolate cake

## 47

**Jarvis** So here's our company cafeteria, Mr Shimura.
**Shimura** It's very nice.
**Jarvis** And there's the menu today.
**Shimura** OK.
**Cafeteria assistant** Hello, can I help you?
**Jarvis** What would you like?
**Shimura** I'd like steak and fries with salad. And mineral water.
**Jarvis** OK. And can I have tomato soup with bread? Oh, and chocolate cake. And I'd like tea.
**Cafeteria assistant** So that's steak and fries, with salad, tomato soup with bread, chocolate cake, mineral water, and tea. That's twenty-three dollars, please.

## 48

Hello, can I help you?
What would you like?
I'd like steak and fries with salad.
And can I have tomato soup with bread?
That's twenty-three dollars, please.

## 49

**Jarvis** Is your lunch OK?
**Shimura** Yes, it's very good. I like steak.
**Jarvis** We have a good cafeteria. What do you normally eat for lunch in Japan?
**Shimura** We eat a lot of rice.
**Jarvis** Do you eat sushi?
**Shimura** *(laughs)* I don't like sushi, but Japanese people eat it.
**Jarvis** Yes, I like Japanese food. Do you like Indian food?
**Shimura** Yes, I do.
**Jarvis** There's a good Indian restaurant in our town. Would you like to go there?

## 50

A What do you do at lunchtime?
B I sing in the company choir.
A Can you sing?
B Yes, I can. Do you want to come?
A No. I can't sing.

## 51

1 play golf
2 play the guitar
3 speak English
4 play tennis
5 run a marathon
6 cook Italian food

## 52

Monday
Tuesday
Wednesday
Thursday
Friday
Saturday
Sunday

## 53

1 It's twelve o'clock.
2 It's three fifteen.
3 It's seven thirty.
4 It's eleven forty-five.

## 54

1 A Do you like Mexican food?
  B Yes, I love it.
  A There's a new Mexican restaurant in town. Would you like to have dinner?
  B Yes, please. That would be nice. What time?
  A Is six OK?
  B I'm afraid I'm busy at six. Is six thirty OK?
  A Sure. See you in reception at six thirty.
2 A Hi. Do you want to play tennis after work?
  B I'd love to, but I can't today.
  A What day can you play?
  B Er … on Thursday?
  A OK. See you on Thursday.
  B That'd be great. Thanks.

## 55

1 A Would you like to play tennis?
  B Yes, that'd be great.
2 A Do you want to play on Friday?
  B I'd love to, but I can't.
3 A What day can you play?
  B On Thursday.
4 A Is six OK?
  B I'm afraid I'm busy at six. Is six thirty OK?

## Unit 7

## 56

**Mustafa** I'm an engineer. I work for an oil company and I manage projects all over the country. In my office, I have a PC and a printer. On site, I have a tablet for notes and a digital camera.

**Julie** I'm a graphic designer in Brisbane, Australia and I work at home. I design websites on my laptop. I have Skype meetings with clients so I need a webcam and headset. I also have a smartphone, of course!

**Andrea** I'm in Sales. I work in an office. Sometimes I travel, and I work in my hotel room or in my car. I have a desktop computer in my office. When I travel, I have my laptop and a small projector with me for presentations. Oh, and my USB stick.

## 57

1 printer
2 USB stick
3 digital camera
4 webcam
5 headset
6 laptop
7 tablet
8 projector
9 smartphone
10 desktop computer

## 58

**Felipe** Hello, Sarah Portman? I'm the new marketing assistant. My name's Felipe Gonzales.
**Sarah** Hi, Felipe. Let me show you round. Right … We have six people in the team. Our project manager is Pierre. He manages key accounts. His office is there. Nadine is our IT manager. She manages the website. Her office is there. And you are in this office. Your desk is here.
**Felipe** Great, thanks.
**Sarah** This is Simone, my PA.
**Simone / Felipe:** Hi.
**Sarah** Olivier and Sandra, our other marketing assistants, aren't here today. They are at a conference. Their desks are over there.
**Felipe** OK.
**Sarah** You have a PC and phone on your desk. Oh, and the printer is here. We all use it. Its 'on' switch is there.
**Felipe** Thanks.
**Sarah** We have a meeting with Sales at ten o'clock so if you …

## 59

A I can't find my laptop.
B Is it on your desk?
A No, it isn't.
B Is it on Pierre's desk?
A No.
B Is it in Remi and Ludo's office?
A No, it isn't there.
B Is it in your manager's office?
A Oh, yes, it is! Thanks.

## 60

**Amanda** What's the problem?
**Ryan** I need to have a video conference with Julie, but I don't know how to use this software. How does it work?
**Amanda** First, you need to enter her name.
**Ryan** OK, so Julie Bamber.
**Amanda** Then click her name.
**Ryan** OK.
**Amanda** Next, click the green video call button.
**Ryan** Oh! She's on the screen. Hello, Julie … Julie? But I can't hear her.
**Amanda** And she can't hear you. Do you have a headset?
**Ryan** Er, no, I don't.
**Amanda** No problem. You can use my headset. You need to connect it to your computer … Does it work now?
**Ryan** Yes, I think so. But she can't hear me.
**Amanda** Is your microphone on?
**Ryan** I don't know. Where do I switch it on?
**Amanda** Just there.
**Julie:** Hi, Ryan.
**Ryan** Yes! Now it works. Hello, Julie. Sorry about that …

## Unit 8

## 61

car
bus
train
bicycle
motorcycle

## 62

1 **Donald** Hello. Can you take me to the airport?
  **Taxi driver** Yes. Which terminal do you want?
  **Donald** Terminal 2.
  …
  **Taxi driver** Here you are. That's eight pounds fifty. Do you want a receipt?
  **Donald** Yes, please.
2 **Donald** Hello. I'm on the Muscat flight.
  **Check-in** Can I have your passport and e-ticket, please?
  **Donald** Here you are.
  **Check-in** Do you have any bags to check in?
  **Donald** Yes. One.
  …
  **Check-in** Here's your passport and your boarding card. Your flight leaves at one o'clock. Please go to the boarding gate at twelve fifteen.
  **Donald** What time does the flight arrive in Muscat?
  **Check-in** Er … at ten forty-five.
  **Donald** Thank you.
  **Check-in** Have a good flight!

## 63

**Alice** Hi, Donald. Where were you yesterday?

**Donald** In Dubai. I was in Oman and the UAE for five days.

**Alice** Oh, yes. How was your trip?

**Donald** OK. Our clients in Muscat were very happy with the new machines.

**Alice** Great! Was Muscat nice?

**Donald** I don't know, because I wasn't there very long. Er … I was in Muscat last Wednesday and Thursday and then there were two meetings in Dubai yesterday. But they weren't very useful. And what about you? Were you busy last week?

**Alice** I wasn't here. I was on holiday.

**Donald** Oh, yes. How was your holiday?

## 64

**Donald** How was your holiday?

**Alice** Great. We were in Barcelona for six days.

**Donald** I was in Barcelona last year. It was a sales conference so it wasn't a holiday. The restaurants were very good, but the city was busy. Were there hundreds of tourists?

**Alice** No, there weren't. It was quiet in the centre.

## 65

January
February
March
April
May
June
July
August
September
October
November
December

## 66

**A** Hi, Anna. Can I check some dates with you?

**B** Yes, of course.

**A** When was your last trip to Turin?

**B** Oh, it was in June – 1st June.

**A** And when is your next trip?

**B** It's in August – 3rd to 14th August.

**A** And the factory visit, when is that?

**B** That's in September – 11th September.

**A** And when's the sales conference?

**B** It's in November. It starts on 27th November and finishes on 30th November.

**A** Thanks for your help.

## 67

1st June
3rd August
14th August
11th September
27th November
30th November

## 68

**Simon** Hi, Ines. It's Simon.

**Ines** Hi, Simon. How can I help?

**Simon** It's about the meeting. Can we arrange a new date and time?

**Ines** Yes, of course.

**Simon** Are you free on Wednesday 31st at 2 p.m.?

**Ines** Sorry, I'm busy. I'm visiting the factory on Tuesday and Wednesday.

**Simon** How about Thursday morning? Are you free then?

**Ines** Yes, I'm free on Thursday morning. What time is good for you?

**Simon** Is 10 a.m. OK for you?

**Ines** Yes, sure. Is the meeting in your office?

**Simon** Yes, it is. See you on Thursday 1st September at 10 a.m. Have a good trip.

**Ines** Thanks.

## 69

1  I'd like to arrange a meeting.
2  I'm free on Tuesday 3rd April.
3  Is 2 p.m. OK for you?
4  How about Friday 11th February?
5  Sorry, I'm busy.
6  The 21st April is fine for me.

## 70

Hi! Don't forget the meeting at head office on 29th April at 9 a.m. Please put the date in your calendar.

UNIVERSITY PRESS

Great Clarendon Street, Oxford, OX2 6DP, United Kingdom

Oxford University Press is a department of the University of Oxford.
It furthers the University's objective of excellence in research, scholarship,
and education by publishing worldwide. Oxford is a registered trade
mark of Oxford University Press in the UK and in certain other countries

ISBN: 978 0 19 473983 2    Book
ISBN: 978 0 19 473981 8    Pack

Printed in China

This book is printed on paper from certified and well-managed sources

ACKNOWLEDGEMENTS

*Illustrations by*: Mark Duffin pp.7, 13 (phone), 41, 44, 66; Leon Mussche pp.14,
23, 46, 64, 67; Nick Lowndes/Eastwing pp.13 (map), 17, 58; Willie Ryan pp.29,
43, 54, 70, 71; Mark Watkinson/Illustration Ltd pp.8, 11, 16, 18, 45, 47, 48, 68.

*The authors and publisher would like to thank the following for their kind permission to
reproduce photographs and other copyright material*: Alamy Images pp.4 (Shaking
hands/Yuri Arcurs), 14 (Customer service representative/DCPhoto), 16 (Coffee
machine/Zoonar GmbH), 17 (Warehouse/Juice Images), 17 (Pentonville Prison/
Photofusion Picture Library), 17 (Office/VIEW Pictures Ltd), 17 (Business Park/
Ashley Cooper), 28 (corporate jet/Martin Williams), 28 (Supermarket shelves/
Kevin Britland), 28 (Samsung Galaxy Note tablet computer/Urbanmyth),
29 (Shirts on clothes rail/Image Source), 30 (Auchan supermarket sign/a la
france), 34 (Pouring water/Shotshop GmbH), 34 (Tandoori chicken masala/Tim
Hill), 34 (Ice cream/UpperCut Images), 34 (Sandwich/Photocuisine), 34 (Orange
juice/Wild Hair Photography), 34 (Black coffee/liv friis-larsen), 34 (Bowl of
Caesar Salad/Stockbroker), 36 (Sophie Walker in golf tournament/Sean Burges/
Mundo Sport Images), 36 (Tennis/Action Plus Sports), 36 (Runners at finish
line/imagebroker), 39 (Empty restaurant/Manor Photography), 39 (Crowded
restaurant/Manor Photography), 40 (Watch clockwork/nobeastofierce), 40 (Ink
jet printer/D. Hurst), 40 (Apple iPad/Oleksiy Maksymenko), 40 (Projector
video/Aigars Reinholds), 40 (Desktop computer/Igor Klimov), 40 (Laptop
computer/David Cook/blueshiftstudios), 42 (Professional man/PhotoAlto),
46 (Huskies/Juniors Bildarchiv GmbH), 51 (Boarding passes/pzechner); Corbis
pp.4 (Adult penguins with chicks/Ralph Lee Hopkins/National Geographic
Society), 5 (Businesswomen shaking hands/Tetra Images), 10 (Office buildings
at night/Rudy Sulgan), 16 (Office building at dusk/Paul Hardy), 21 (Overpass
interchange/Cameron Davidson), 24 (Businesswoman giving presentation/Phil
Boorman/cultura), 28 (Visitors in car showroom/Kiyoshi Ota/X02055/Reuters),
30 (LG electronics factory/Andrew Kent), 36 (Woman talking on phone/
Tetra Images), 36 (Man preparing meal/Image Source), 45 (Computer chip
and circuit board/Andrew Brookes); EE p.36 (EE company choir); Fred
Meesmaecker p.22 (Fred Meesmaecker); Getty Images pp.4 (Business people
shaking hands/Stockbyte), 5 (Man repairing computer/Tetra Images),
5 (Businesswoman with laptop/Alex Mares-Manton), 5 (Office worker/Lava),
5 (Businessman on phone/Lane Oatey/Blue Jean Images), 6 (Business people
talking/RelaxFoto.de), 9 (Zebras/Gallo Images – Nigel Dennis), 10 (Business
card exchange/altrendo images), 12 (Rio de Janeiro/luoman), 15 (Businessmen
talking/Erik Isakson), 16 (Businessman working on laptop/Stigur Karlsson),
16 (Gated business/Tony Tremblay), 17 (Woman at reception/Zero Creatives),
22 (Rice paddy fields/Pete Atkinson), 27 (Birds sitting on wire/Spangles44
flickr), 28 (Colourful ethnic clothing/Lynn Gail), 28 (Molikpaq offshore
oil platform/Ursula Hyzy/AFP), 29 (aeroplane assembly/Pauko Fridman/
Bloomberg), 33 (Journalists microphones/Franck Fife/AFP),
34 (Victoria Derby Day/Mark Dadswell), 34 (Vegetable lasagne/Robert
Linton), 34 (Tomato soup and bread/J Shepherd/Photodisc), 34 (Chocolate
truffle cake/Sarah K. Lee), 35 (Business lunch/Pinnacle Pictures/Digital
Vision), 44 (Video call/Image Source); Masterfile p.17 (Factory production
line/Boden/Ledingham); Oxford University Press pp.32 (Cardboard boxes/
RTimages), 34 (Tea/Amana Images Inc.), 40 (Digital Camera/Alamy Creativity);
Shutterstock pp.5 (Engineer/Viktor Gladkov), 13 (Male office worker/
StockLite), 13 (Smiling businesswoman/Robert Kneschke), 13 (Businesswoman/
Stuart Jenner), 13 (Portrait of businessman/Andresr), 13 (Businessman with
arms folded/hfng), 13 (Businesswoman with digital tablet/Robert Kneschke),
22 (Woman working in office/Andresr), 34 (Steak and chips/ilolab), 36 (Girl
playing guitar/muratart), 40 (Smartphone/Umberto Shtanzman), 40 (USB stick/
Aaron Amat), 40 (Webcam/Blazej Lyjak), 40 (Headset/Shyamalamuralinath).

*Cover image by*: Getty Images (Businesswoman with laptop/Echo)

*The authors and publisher are grateful to those who have given permission to reproduce
the following extract and adaptation of copyright material*: p.22 Information about
Fred Meesmaecker. Reproduced by kind permission of Fred Meesmaecker.

*Sources*: p.46 www.japan-guide.com

*The authors and publisher would also like to thank the following individuals for their
advice and assistance in developing the material for this book*: Maira Bertante,
Susie Oswald, Pat Pledger, Graeme Romanes.